JIM CRAMER'S

MAD MONEY

WATCH TV, GET RICH

JAMES J. CRAMER
WITH CLIFF MASON

Simon & Schuster
New York London Toronto Sydney

SIMON & SCHUSTER
Rockefeller Center
1230 Avenue of the Americas
New York, NY 10020

SIMON & SCHUSTER and colophon are registered trademarks
of Simon & Schuster, Inc.

Designed by Elliott Beard

Manufactured in the United States of America

1   3   5   7   9   10   8   6   4   2

Library of Congress Cataloging-in-Publication Data is available.

ISBN-13: 978-1-4165-3790-8
ISBN-10: 1-4165-3790-2

For information about special discounts for bulk purchases,
please contact Simon & Schuster Special Sales:
1-800-456-6798 or business@simonandschuster.com

To our respective mothers,
Louise Cramer and Nan Cramer Mason

CONTENTS

MAD MONEY

Investing well isn't easy, but it is possible. My goal in life is to make it easier for you to make money. I want to help out regular people with paying a mortgage, or college tuition, or hey, if we really do well, maybe buying a boat. Picking the right stocks is one of the hardest parts of investing, and every night on *Mad Money,* I try to take some of that burden off your shoulders. If you watch the show, I can give you good stocks. I can help you understand where the market's going. My last book, *Jim Cramer's Real Money: Sane Investing in an Insane World,* gave you the disciplines and insights I had developed over the course of my long career as a money manager. Since I wrote *Real Money,* it's gotten harder to be a regular investor. We live in a more dynamic, more economically integrated world, and that means it takes more effort to know all the facts you need to invest wisely. In this book, I'll show you how you can best use *Mad Money* to make money in this new, more complex global economy, and I'll also teach you the many new lessons about investing that I've learned from putting the show together every weekday for more than a year. I hope *Mad Money,* and this *Mad Money* book, can give you a life that's richer in wealth if not necessarily in spirit.

But if you think just watching *Mad Money* alone can make you rich, you're dead wrong. If you think that watching the show and maybe doing a little research on the side can make you money, I'd bet you're off the mark there too. It's not enough just to process what I say on the show. You need to know what to do with it. And that, my friends, is what this book is all about.

I want to help you take the advice I give out on *Mad Money* and show you how you can turn that advice into money in your pocket. That's what I'm all about: helping everybody get rich. There's a method you need to use, there are protocols to follow. Sometimes you'll need a translator to understand what I'm saying on the show, because I get a little caught up with the idea of being on TV and start making lots of incomprehensible references to things only a few hundred people have ever heard of. But if you watch the show, and if you use this book to turn my advice on the show into real investment strategies, I think you'll be able to make yourself some serious dough. I don't want to knock the show—it's fun to watch—but there's more to investing than I can convey in an hour a night of TV, especially when I have to keep from being too didactic in order to hold everybody's attention.

This book is about maximizing what you can do with the market advice I freely distribute on the show—advice that comes out of two decades of experience playing the market, and playing to win. This book is the necessary complement to *Mad Money,* and the even more necessary sequel to *Jim Cramer's Real Money: Sane Investing in an Insane World.* In *Real Money* I wanted to help individual investors make money in the stock market. I wrote that book before I had *Mad Money,* and in the last year and a half, things have changed. I learned more in the first year of making my show than I learned in any five years I spent running my hedge fund. Now I've got a new approach to stocks. It's pretty simple: there's no such thing as the market. Whenever people talk about "the market," they're really talking about a very small group of large institutions: hedge funds and mutual funds. Because these funds control so much of the money in the market, they're the ones who determine stock prices. A stock is only worth what the big institutions are willing to pay for it. *Mad Money* and this book are both meant to help you, the individual investor, understand what these big players are doing and to help you try to beat them at their own game. In this book, I'll tell you how to make the best use of my show in light of my new philosophy, and I'll teach you the important new lessons I've learned since I wrote *Real Money*. The market's changed; my new rules will help you capitalize on my most recent experience with stocks, and they'll help you deal with a stock market that's gotten harder.

Now, sometimes I've got to toot my own horn just so you guys will listen to me. I have a few talents: I am a pretty good stock picker and a successful investor. Just so you don't think I'm conceited, I'm also not the most considerate guy on earth, and I'm a bad sport when playing Monopoly. The point is, I know how to make money in the market, and I want to help you make as much money as possible. I'm not doing it to be famous, and I'm not doing it for the pay, because I've already got more money than I feel comfortable having, and I say that as an incredibly greedy capitalist. I *need* to make you rich. I don't know why, maybe it's out of a pervasive sense of guilt, maybe I'm a nice guy—it doesn't matter. You will need more than just *Mad Money* if you're going to make the money I want you to make.

Originally, back at the end of 2004 when we first started throwing ideas together to make the show, I had a plan. There are a lot of people out there who need reliable, honest advice about stocks. You can't be sure about research from this or that brokerage house. They've all been tarnished; they've been tarred and feathered and ridden out of town on a rail for colluding with their clients. And business journalism has the same problem as every other kind of journalism. Nobody ever takes a side, expresses an opinion, or even evaluates the validity of the press releases they get. No one ever puts his neck in doctor guillotine. Instead, they present these bland pseudo-analyses that in the end tell you nothing. Reporters want to tell you the news. You can't make a dime off the news unless you know what to do with it, and that's why *Mad Money* was born. I wanted to do something different and more helpful.

My goal is to create hundreds of thousands, maybe millions of people who diligently invest their money in stocks and come out of it with some mad money. I happen to think my TV show is great. I think it's the best thing on TV short of *24, The Shield,* and most of what's on HBO. Good as I think it is, you need more. You need a supplement, you need something that lets you convert what I give you on the show into money in your pocket, and that's why you need this book.

Here's how it all comes together. I may play a total madman on TV, but I'm really just a very unbalanced guy at home. However, when it comes to stocks, I believe in being rigorous and methodical, not crazy. There's no madness to my method. If you want to watch *Mad Money* and then turn around and make yourself a fortune, you have to understand that method. You have to know what to watch for—which observations are significant and which ones aren't.

That's the way this book will make you money. The great thing about *Mad Money* is that it's an up-to-the-minute show. *Real Money,* my last book, has great general advice about the strategies you should be using to make money in the market, but it has no up-to-the-minute, immediate component. What you're getting in this book is a way to take the detailed, immediate recommendations and observations from the show and turn them into money in your pocket.

I want this book to guide you through the nitty-gritty details of researching the stocks I recommend every single night on the show. I don't just hand you money on a silver platter. I wish I could. I wish it grew on trees, but it takes hard work to make money. I think I'm giving great advice on the show, but you still have to do your homework if you're going to turn that advice into the one thing we're after: money. So in this book, I'll tell you how to do the homework and how to decide which stocks are for you and which stocks you should stay away from, given your age or your personality. I want to guide you through the process of purchasing the stocks you like and then deciding when, where, and how to sell those stocks. I never have time to get into this sort of thing on the show, but it's just as important to know how to buy and sell the right stocks as it is to know how to pick them. I want to take some of the more complicated concepts and ideas that I use on the show and break them down for you, because knowing how to decode genuine Wall Street gibberish, and genuine Cramer gibberish, will improve your game.

I'm writing this book because I want you to feel like you've got me sitting right next to you, guiding you every step of the way when you buy and sell the stocks I pick on the show, or when you just try to implement my more general advice. But I want to do more with this handbook than just teach you how to follow my marching orders. Just as I do on the show, I want to educate you. Making *Mad Money* has been an education for me, and I have twenty new rules for investing, rules that I've formulated by rigorously analyzing my successes and failures. These rules explain how to invest in a market where the big hedge funds and mutual funds run the show. They're new disciplines that will let you anticipate the behavior of the big institutions. If you can do that, you can get rich. I'm not repudiating my rules in *Real Money*—they're still valid—but the world has changed. My twenty new rules are a supplement to my *Real Money* rules, not a substitute for them.

That's not all. If you want to get the most out of *Mad Money*, you need to understand how I operate. Every night I take dozens of calls in the "Lightning Round," a segment where callers ask me what I think about their stocks. I don't know what the stocks will be beforehand, but I still manage to give out decent advice. In this book, I'll show you exactly how I can tell people whether to buy or sell something with only five or ten seconds to think about the stock. I'm revealing all the secrets of the "Lightning Round" and all the tricks I use to pull it off every night. Not only that, I'll even show you how to do your own Lightning Round—not in order to impress your friends, but because the preparation necessary for a good Lightning Round may be the best way for you to sharpen your stock-picking and investment skills. It's stock market strength training.

Almost every night, I interview a different CEO or CFO on the show. A lot of people tune out for those interviews because they don't think they can get anything out of them. In this book, I'll tell you exactly how to watch my CEO interviews because they're an incredibly useful asset—but they're an asset you have to learn how to exploit.

I know that many people want to game the show. You want to be able to figure out what I'm going to say before I say it, because the show moves stocks. You want a trick that will let you read my mind so you can buy stocks *before* I recommend them. I'll tell you straight out: there is no trick. There's no real way to game the show. But you can learn how to think like me. I'll tell you some of the ways I pick stocks for the show. You'll get a glimpse of my thought process as I try to put together good picks that I think will make you money. If you know how I pick stocks for the show, you probably still won't be able to anticipate *Mad Money*'s recommendations. But you will learn how I decide which stocks to feature, and that's not a bad thing to know.

I may be a good stock picker, but I'll admit that I'm not the most polished broadcaster on earth, and sometimes I can be, let's say, incomprehensible. That's why I'm giving you a guide to all the weird terms I use and some of the esoteric, even obnoxious cultural references I make. Can this stuff make you money? If you think hard enough, probably. But the real point is that it makes watching the show more fun, and if watching the show is fun, then investing will be fun. As long as you enjoy investing, you'll be willing to do the homework and stay in the game. That's why I try to make the show so entertaining, because if you aren't interested, you'll either miss the opportunity to make money in the market or not pay enough attention and end up losing your shirt.

And in the interest of keeping things fun—because again, where there's no fun, there's won't be any money (hey, the reverse is true too)—I've got a glossary that explains all my props and, even better, my sound effects and what they're supposed to mean. I want you to know what you should do when I push a given button. It's a science: it's Cramerology.

At the end of the book, I give you a stock worksheet that will help you keep track of all the steps you need to take if you want to own a stock. The worksheet is a template, a way to organize your thoughts so that you can follow the instructions I lay out in the first part of this book for buying and selling stocks. You don't have to use the worksheet, but if it helps even just a little bit, then why not?

I'll try anything to help make you wealthier than you are—you know that if you've ever seen the show. I just can't stop myself; I'm addicted to making you money. I should be spending all day in a country club or never getting out of my pajamas like Hugh Hefner. But here I am, writing this *Mad Money* book, because I have a categorical imperative to help you get rich, and the show is not enough. I hope you enjoy it, and I hope it helps you get that house or that car. Or, let's get really ambitious and try for the yacht.

1

BUYING A STOCK
MAD MONEY STYLE

Step One:
Know Yourself and Your Goals

Let's cut to the chase. I come out on my show and I tell you to buy a stock. I give it a big, triple-buy, I give you the whole shtick about why it's great and why you should own it. What should your response be?

Well, if you really want to get the most out of *Mad Money,* and I'm not talking about literary value here, or even entertainment value, you need a pretty good understanding of who you are, where you are in your life, and what you're after. I don't want this to be a self-help book. The last thing in the world I want is to turn into the Dr. Phil of investment advice. But if you don't know what your priorities are—and I can give you an idea of what they should be if you need help in that department—then trying to invest will be a lot harder than it should be, and *Mad Money,* for all its virtues, won't help you at all.

When I recommend a stock on *Mad Money,* I don't have time to go through exactly what type of person should own that stock. And even if I did have time, the legal department at CNBC has some problems with my giving out individualized investment advice. That's why I'm devoting some space in this book to helping you figure out what kind of investor you want to be. That way, when you watch the show, you can have a perspective that will not only help you make money, but, beyond that, will let you measure your own successes and failures. Let me give you a quick example. If I tell you to buy a stock that I believe will double over the next eighteen months, and you really just want to make some quick trades that will give you smaller but quicker gains, you shouldn't buy that stock. You won't get what you're after, and when you don't get what you're after, I get angry e-mails. So let's do our best right now to set you up for success at whatever it is you're trying to do. The goal is always to make you mad money, but there are different ways to do it, and mad money doesn't mean the same thing at twenty-five that it means at fifty or seventy-five. I want you to figure out where you're coming from. Maybe you think this is intuitive, that you have a visceral sense of your goals and your financial position, but it pays to be careful.

A lot of people who are trying to make money in the market don't have a sense of their own identity as investors. Some people *think* they do. I've made this mistake countless times, which is why I'm the guy to help make sure you don't. Before you watch the show and try to take my advice, you need to ask yourself a set of questions, and I'll lay them out right here.

First and foremost, how old are you? If I come out on the show and recommend Conexant (CNXT), which when I first came out in favor of it was a debt-laden, under-two-dollar speculative company that made parts for television set-top boxes, I'm not necessarily recommending the stock for *you*. As it happened, Conexant could have made some people a lot of money in a very short time. I got behind it on September 19, 2005, at a buck sixty-three a share, and four months later, on January 19, it closed at three dollars and thirty-four cents a share. Now, even though I got that one right, that was not a stock that you should've put any retirement savings into. It's not a stock that I would recommend a sixty-year-old buy, unless he or she happens to have a whole lot of extra money to put on the table and risk losing.

Some of you are probably saying to yourselves, money is money. Why should it make any difference how old I am if stocks like Conexant can deliver that kind of return? In most things I'm an egalitarian. I think that in all the important, essential ways, people are the same. But when it comes to money, you have to deal with some upsetting realities. We are not all financially equal. And not all stocks are equally risky. The young, I hate to admit at the ripe old age of fifty-one, are allowed to take a lot more risks with their money than the middle-aged or the elderly. And when it comes to money, this is the one place where it's not smart to lie about your age, although to look youthful I often claim I am sixty-two years old on air. It's not that young people are better at managing risk. The odds are good that if you're a young investor, you don't have the experience to manage risk as well as someone who's a bit more seasoned. In a way, it's ironic that young people, who have the least experience, also have the most latitude in how they can invest. It's ironic, but as far as I'm concerned, it's also financial gospel.

Young people can take more risks with their money, because they can afford to lose more money. If you've got more time to earn back your losses, you can afford to take bigger risks. A risky stock like Conexant is perfect for someone just out of college. You can count on me to give you honest and good advice, but I'll get it wrong sometimes, and when I do, if you're acting on my recommendations, it's possible you'll lose money. If I were in your shoes, I'd rather lose money as a recent college grad, who has a whole career to earn it back, than as a retiree who's depending on that income for rent, or medical bills, or food, or yacht fuel. That's why, on my "Back to School" tour, I offer college kids some of the riskiest alternatives out there. That doesn't mean you can't make money as you get older; it just means you should pay more attention to my conservative stock picks and a lot less attention to the sexy-looking speculative ones.

How old are you? is the first question that'll determine the way you approach my show and the way you should approach the market. It's a rude question, but making money can be a rude business. The second question, a two-parter, frankly is even more obnoxious: how much money do you have in the bank, and what's your income? I tell people never to put more than 20 percent of their discretionary money, which means the money that they're not saving for retirement, into speculative stocks. Those are the risky stocks like Conexant that can deliver the big gains or the big losses. That's a rule, and it's one I'm sticking to because I'm a law-and-order kind of guy. But to be honest, if you're really rich, if you're raking in a lot of money, you can afford to speculate with half or even all of your investment income. I don't recommend it. I don't think it's smart. You only need to get rich once. But this is another uncomfortable truth that has to be acknowledged: the richer you are, the less you need to worry about money. It's obvious on a gut level, but no one likes to be told that they don't make enough money to be taking real risks in the market.

It is a question of risk. Losing money means nothing to the really rich, so they can be more aggressive. The money you are investing is meant to increase your wealth, and it would be imprudent to take *extra* risk if you have less.

If you don't have a lot of money to invest with and you're approaching retirement, don't put your money in risky stuff. I get behind risky stocks all the time on the show, but they're meant only for people who have either the time or the money to be able to afford the risk. I want to make you rich, but I've got my own Hippocratic oath, and the first step to making you rich is keeping you from becoming poor. You can make money in stocks at any age, even with very little money. But you have to use different strategies depending on how old you are and how much you've got in the bank. In terms of how much money you should have if you want to start investing in stocks, I've always said you should have ten thousand dollars that you can afford to put into stocks. That's separate from retirement money. You can still make money with five thousand dollars, or even less than that, but once you get too low, even today's small commissions will eat into your profits, and the amount of effort necessary to beat the market won't end up providing you with commensurate gains.

We've gone over your age and your bank account—not fun subjects, not polite subjects, but even when it's fun, making money is a serious game, no matter what kind of stunts I pull on my show. There are two more things you need to know about yourself before I'll let you approach my show as a serious investor. This stuff is a lot less touchy. You need to know your temperament. There's a certain level of calm that everyone needs to have to beat the market, but I've yet to meet anyone who couldn't relax enough to make money in stocks. You have to keep yourself distanced from the bad days, because sometimes you lose. Some people are just born more comfortable taking risks than others. Some of us are conservative, and despite how I act on the show, I'm actually a pretty conservative investor. I don't want you to lie to yourself here—and I know this sounds like New Age garbage, but please bear with me, because I promise this is something that can make you rich. A lot of people who invest feel pressure to take bigger risks than they're comfortable taking; we live in a culture that celebrates risk taking. We love cowboys, and even though there haven't been more than a couple of decent Westerns made in the last fifteen years, this is still true.

I'm here to tell you that it's OK, when you watch my show, to write off all the speculative, under-ten-dollar, unprofitable, risky stocks I recommend if you don't feel right about buying them. It's OK to feel some trepidation at taking big risks, and if you aren't comfortable, you won't have fun if you do. When you don't have fun, you aren't as motivated to do the work, and when you ain't motivated, you ain't making money. That's half the point of my show. So please, I beg you, if you're not a big risk taker, just forget about the speculative stocks. There's nothing wrong with wanting to own big, solid, dividend-paying, stable companies. You can make of a lot of money that way, and you won't have to pull your hair out worrying about the risk. Let me tell you, at my hedge fund I would take risks that I didn't necessarily feel good about, and if I'd been more of a gunslinger at heart, I'd probably have a little more hair on my head today.

We've got age, income, and personality. The last question, before I let you listen to my stock picks, is about your priorities. And this is pretty simple stuff. Are you in the game for the long haul, do you want stocks that are going to make you money in the next year, or are you after trades that will make you money in the next week? I try to have something for everybody. *Mad Money* has been chock full of good trades, and I've also given you some great investments—not to ignore the mistakes I've made along the way. If you want to trade, you need more free time. I don't believe in buying a stock and holding it—you know, if you've seen the show, that you've gotta do at least one hour of homework a week per stock you own. But if you really want to trade some of my picks, that's more labor intensive. The shorter your time horizons for making money, the more time and effort you must put into the homework. I know people have said that my show is for traders and not longer-term investors, but the truth is that *Mad Money* is most useful for people who don't have a ton of free time to trade in. Again, I try to play Zero Mostel in *A Funny Thing Happened on the Way to the Forum* and have something for everyone, but if you're day trading, look, *Mad Money* is only an hour of show a day, and it comes on after the close. That means I have a lot less to offer you.

I went over a risky, speculative stock already, Conexant, but there are three other classes of good stocks worth owning that I want to go over with you so that you can easily identify them on the show and pick out the ones that are right for you. The other three types of good stocks, as opposed to bad stocks that will lose you money, are stocks with high growth, stocks with consistent growth, and value stocks. On the show I will try to identify every single stock I recommend as falling into one of these categories. High-growth stocks, obviously, have high growth, but that's not their only characteristic. These are the riskiest of the three types of nonspeculative stocks. As with almost everything involving money, more risk means more reward. High-growth stocks can make you a lot of money because the fund managers on Wall Street live for growth, and they adore any stock that can deliver really high growth. And by high growth, I'm talking about any stock that's growing its earnings at 20 percent or more annually. As long as these stocks keep delivering, they'll make you money, but it's not all milk and honey here. If a high-growth stock fails to deliver, if it disappoints the Street by reporting earnings that are a little shy of expectations or growth that's a little lower than what the Street wants, the stock will get crushed, even though in the case of great franchises like Starbucks or Whole Foods Market, they can bounce back. Sooner or later this happens to every high-growth stock, because a company can become only so big, and the bigger you are, the harder it is to grow. My sister's father-in-law was a crop duster, and he'd always say that there are two kinds of pilots: the ones who have crashed, and the ones who are going to crash. It's no different with high-growth stocks.

Don't get me wrong—with a little homework, you'll be able to avoid getting seriously hurt in high-growth names. But they're more risky than consistent growers or value stocks, and you need to take that into account when you're trying to set up a portfolio that's right for you. Because consistent growers are less risky, unsurprisingly, they don't tend to make you as much money. But they have other good qualities that make up for the fact that they go up less. Here I'm really talking about stocks like PepsiCo (PEP) or General Mills (GIS). Consistent growers pay out dividends. I love dividends. What could be better than having a company hand you money for doing nothing other than owning the stock? I know, some of the daredevils out there will scoff—as I write this PepsiCo pays out a 2-percent dividend and General Mills a 2.7-percent dividend. It's not a lot of money, I'll admit. But if you're aiming to make yourself a 7 to 10 percent gain in the market, which is beyond respectable for a conservative portfolio, or even a risky one, that dividend money will definitely help you get there. Consistent growers are very shareholder friendly: they don't just pay dividends, they also tend to buy back stock. This helps you out in two ways. First, by decreasing the number of shares out there, these companies increase the earnings per share and make your shares more valuable. That's the reason companies do buybacks. The second great thing about a buyback is that when anyone, including the company the stock belongs to, buys large amounts of stock, the stock goes up because buybacks tighten supply. In a bad market where no one wants to buy stocks, having the company there with a buyback in place creates an automatic buyer and keeps the stock from getting hit too hard. You can think of it as a cushion or a parachute effect, and it will keep you from getting discouraged in a bad market. These stocks probably couldn't have done anything for my hairline, but truth be told, I just shave my head because women seem to love it.

Value stocks are the third and most conservative kind of stock worth owning. All value stocks are cheap, but not all cheap stocks have value. Actually, let's not call value stocks cheap. Value stocks are inexpensive; they're low priced. Bad stocks are cheap. With a good value stock, you're getting great merchandise that's been put on sale for bad reasons, not shoddy merchandise that's been marked down because it's not worth very much. On *Mad Money*, when I go for value, I usually do a pretty good job of separating the wheat from the chaff. Value stocks often pay high-yielding dividends, not because the companies have nothing to do with their cash, but because they've gone so low that regular large-sized dividends turn into humongous ones. Not all value stocks pay dividends. Some are companies that, when you look at their underlying assets, are just priced way too low for bad reasons. I'll tell you all about valuation later on; right now I just want to give you a feel for the different breeds of stocks. Value stocks have usually come down for a reason, that reason being either something bad about the company or its sector or something irrational about the market. If you're going to buy value stocks, you want to be sure that they'll go up. Value investors have a longer time frame than growth investors, but it's not an infinite time frame. On the show, I don't recommend value stocks unless I can explain to you why they're going to come up. And you're not allowed to buy any stocks unless you can explain to a friend who knows nothing about the market why that stock is going higher.

A good example of a value stock—again, as I write this book; it may not be a value stock when you read this—is Walter Industries (WLT), which I talked about on *Mad Money* on June 23, 2006. At the time, Walter was a value stock because of the huge discrepancy between its value and the value of its underlying assets. Walter was a $2-billion company with a number of different businesses. It produced high-quality coal, the kind you use to make steel; it had a home-building business; and it also owned 85.5 million shares of a company called Mueller Water Products (MWA). When I recommended Walter, that position in Mueller was worth $1.3 billion. That meant the market was valuing Walter's coal and home-building businesses at just $700 million, and that was way too cheap. Walter became inexpensive because it had been beaten up during May 2006, a really terrible month for stocks. But even before it fell to 48.39, where it was when I recommended it, the stock was cheap. When I talked about Walter on the show, it was trading at less than nine times expected 2006 earnings, even though it was expected to have 20 percent growth going forward. It had a P/E of 8.8 and a PEG rate of just 0.44. (I'll define these terms more thoroughly when I tell you about the homework you should do on a stock in just a little bit.) Take my word for the moment, those two numbers made this stock inexpensive based on the value of its assets and its growth, and that's what makes a great value stock, that's what makes it a gift if it goes lower.

There's no reason that you can't own speculative stocks, high-growth stocks, consistent-growth stocks, and value stocks all at the same time. The name of the game is diversification—you *want* to own different kinds of stocks. But, depending on those variables we talked about before—age, wealth, personality—you'll want to own different amounts of each kind of stock. If you're conservative, you want more value, more consistent growth, and less high growth, with maybe no speculation at all. If you're young and love to skydive, you'll want to own a speculative name and high-growth stocks, but you still should have some consistent growers and value stocks, just not as much exposure as someone who's more risk averse.

Now that you've taken a good look at how old you are, how much money you have, what kind of temperament you're saddled with, and what, given those three things, your investment goals are, you can get down to the business of watching *Mad Money* and trying to turn my advice into stock-market gold. If you know yourself, you'll know which stocks are for you. But if you want to buy a *Mad Money* stock, something I've pitched, then I'd really appreciate it, and I think your wallet would appreciate it, too, if you followed my standard operating procedure for researching, buying, and then selling stocks.

2

BUYING A STOCK
MAD MONEY STYLE

Step Two:
Do Your Homework

If there's one thing that makes me really, really furious, it's going into a bar and not being recognized by a single person there even though I've got a national TV show. But if we can count two things that make me mad, the second one has to be this: whenever I mention a stock on the show and some misguided individual—I would have said something much less polite if I weren't such an elder-statesman figure now—immediately goes out in after-hours trading and buys that stock, placing a market order, not a limit order, as I demand. That misguided fellow is about to lose some serious money. And I'm all about making money, not losing it.

I want to put a stop to this behavior once and for all. I'm going to put the fear of Cramer into you. If you even so much as think of immediately buying a stock in after-hours trading when I recommend it, know this: there are hundreds if not thousands of professional traders poised to tear you to pieces and rob you blind. They're sitting there, waiting for someone like you to come in and put in a market order for a stock. These guys, if they're anything like I was—and they are, otherwise they wouldn't be making money—they're going to short you the stock. Shorting is when you borrow a stock, sell it to someone, and then—if you do it right—buy it back at a lower price and keep the difference between where you sold it and where you bought it back. Let me give you a quick example to help make this clear, because shorting stock is one of those things that can look very complicated when you explain it theoretically, but actually is very simple if you just watch how it works. I want to decode all the Wall Street gibberish out there, so I don't want to break my own rules by mentioning something in passing without breaking it down to the basics.

Let's say I'm one of these short-sellers, these jackals who just want you to make a wrong step so they can rob you blind. What am I doing precisely? For the sake of the example, let's say I'm shorting Vonage (VG), the Internet telephone company, also commonly referred to as "the dog" on *Mad Money*. That means I'm betting Vonage will go down, but that doesn't explain the mechanics, which is what you need to know. If I were at my hedge fund, in order to short Vonage, I would call up my broker, and tell him that I want to sell a hundred shares of Vonage short at $15 a share. My broker would then go out and borrow those shares. Don't worry about whom he's borrowing them from; the big investment banks sit on a hoard of stock that they can lend out to short sellers. So he borrows the stock for me, and then he sells it at $15 a share. Now I've got $1,500 from that sale. I wait for Vonage to come down, let's say to $10 because Vonage was a real underperformer after it came public. Then I "cover" my short. That means I take $1,000 because now the stock is at $10, and buy back those hundred shares of Vonage that I initially borrowed. The shares get returned to whomever the broker borrowed them from, and I'm left with $500. My profit from shorting Vonage comes from the difference between where I sold it after I borrowed it and the amount I had to pay to "cover"—to buy back that stock I initially borrowed. I sold Vonage high, at $15 a share, and bought it back low, at $10. It might help to think of shorting as regular investing in reverse—sell high, buy low.

Now that we've gone over what these short sellers do, let me explain how it will hurt you if you don't follow my advice to never, ever buy stock after hours. We're back to after-hours trading, right after I've recommended a stock on *Mad Money*. When you try to buy stock after hours, there's very little stock out there because all the exchanges are closed. Only short sellers who want to destroy you will sell the stock, and they'll sell it at a price even the Mafia would cringe at charging. They can get away with charging you that price because you put in a market order, and a market order gives your broker, who just wants to earn his commission, license to pay anything. Because they're borrowing the stock, the shorts are the only ones with a real supply of stock to sell after hours. So they watch the show, wait for a stock to pop, and then sell you the stock really high after hours. Then, the next day, at around 10:00 to 11:00 a.m., when the stock starts to decline and you get discouraged about having bought it so high, so you boot it, the shorts will cover—that means buy back the stock they borrowed and return it—and make a fortune while you lose money. I want you to stop buying stocks in after-hours trading, period. I want you never to use a market order again, period. I don't want you to be fodder for these people. I'm going to do my best in this book and on the show to prevent you from being torn to shreds by the vultures who circle *Mad Money*, waiting for unsuspecting investors to make a fatal financial mistake so they can feed.

But better than that, better for you, because most of you are smart and don't just leap all over my picks as soon as I recommend them, I want to tell you exactly what to do in the first twenty-four hours after I recommend a stock. If people can't make good use of my recommendations on the show, I might as well just pack up, quit, and move to Tahiti, where it's always sunny. I live in New Jersey so I can tape

Mad Money in CNBC's Jersey studio. Do you have any idea what kind of sacrifice I'm making in order to do that? And I *like* Jersey. I grew up in Philadelphia, who am I to complain? Again, the point here is that if you don't know what to do with my recommendations, if you aren't in a position to execute the trades I'm advising in the best possible way, it's going to be much harder for you to make money, and making you money is the name of the game.

Now, since you're prepared to sort through my stock picks and find the ones that fit your risk profile—I know that sounds like such a terrible term, like the kind of thing you'd hear from an insurance company, not me, but the term fits the bill—we can go into the market and buy Cramer's stock tips, right?

Oh, no. Big mistake, my friends. First of all, I don't give out stock tips on my show. That's the Fifth Commandment of trading in *Jim Cramer's Real Money: Sane Investing in an Insane World*—tips are for waiters. Tips are either meaningless and useless, or they're illegal. I give you analysis. I highlight stocks that I think are high quality, stocks that I believe can make you money. But you know what, it doesn't matter what I think. It matters what *you* think. *Mad Money* is a tool; it's a bridge to making you a better investor, to making you more money. But I'm not the supreme arbiter of all things stock related, and you can't treat the show as if it'll be 100 percent right all the time. I said I would tell you what to do the first twenty-four hours after the show and that's exactly what I'm about to do.

When I recommend a stock on the show and it really catches your eye, and you think it works for you, there's one thing you're absolutely not allowed to do in the first twenty-four hours, unless you've really got some spare time and a lot of energy. In the first day after I tell you to buy a stock, and you like that stock, you are absolutely forbidden to buy it. That's a new rule I'm coining right here. Forget after-hours trading, I don't even want you buying the stock the next day. There are a lot of reasons for this, and since it seems a little crazy for me to be telling you that yes means no and no means yes, I'll go over them.

First of all, just as when a big Wall Street research firm upgrades a stock—it's really no different—a lot of people jump to buy stocks after I recommend them. And when you get a lot of buyers, it's just simple economics that the stock will go up. People have been calling this the Cramer effect, but it's really not unique to me at all, or even all that interesting. If Stacy Pak, who's the great retail analyst over at Prudential, upgrades a stock, it goes up because people listen to her advice and buy it. But nobody calls that the Pak effect, and frankly, I think the Pak effect sounds a lot cooler than the Cramer effect, like something in a science-fiction movie. Just as I would never tell you to buy a stock right on the heels of an analyst upgrade, unless it was really, really right and the stock had a lot more upside, I'd never tell you to buy right on the heels of a Cramer upgrade.

So if you can't buy the stock in the first day—and honestly, I might suggest giving it a week or even two to find a good entry point—what should you be doing in that first twenty-four hours after I hook you on a great-sounding stock? My friends, I know you hate the sound of this, but those first twenty-four hours are for homework. Not all of them, obviously—you can still sleep and eat and go to work, although when I get into a stock, I sometimes forget about all that mundane stuff. You don't have to spend a whole day on homework, or anything like that, before you're allowed to buy, but you must do the work. And that means I have to tell you what homework is.

You're watching *Mad Money,* eyes on fire with rapt attention, or something like that, and I tell you to buy a stock. First, hear me out. I joke about taking out a pencil and paper, but to be honest, it's not such a bad idea to jot down the key points I'm making in favor of the stock. You want to make sure you understand the rationale for owning the thing. Once a stock catches your eye, you need to do some homework. I know, owning stocks isn't all booyahs and excitement, but trust me, if you do the homework right, you'll be plenty happy, and there'll be plenty of big, *Mad Money* booyahs all around. Your actual homework is fairly simple. Once a stock catches your interest, go look it up on the Internet. I don't care if you use Yahoo! Finance, or the *Wall Street Journal Online,* or TheStreet.com, which is my company. (I actually do feel a little hesitant to recommend my company, because despite my general shamelessness, I still believe in some degree of propriety.)

So what should you be looking for? You'll see the price highlighted in bold, but that's relatively unimportant. If you're considering buying a stock, you're going to want to examine a number of things. First of all, you're coming into the situation with a thesis, fully formed, straight from *Mad Money.* But let's put aside my thesis for a second, and instead do the standard homework that you would do for any stock. There are a lot of things for you to look at, but I find it's easier to do homework if we define our tasks in terms of their purpose. I could tell you to look at the 10-K—that's the annual report a company has to file with the Securities and Exchange Commission (SEC) that provides a really comprehensive overview of the business—and listen to or read transcripts of the conference calls, or look over the balance sheet. All of these are elements of homework, but they're totally meaningless unless you know why you're doing them.

In general, when you do homework you're really trying to figure out only a few things about a stock. I want to lay out the whole process in a set of easy steps so that you can easily figure out these things and know when you've completed the work. There are five steps to the homework that you should do before buying one of the stocks I recommend, or any stock for that matter. In the back of this book, there is a worksheet where you can write down all of the information you get from doing each step. Whenever a stock I talk about on the show really grabs you, and you think it's the right fit for your style of investing, you should go to the worksheet and do the homework. I know I'm beating the homework theme to death, and the worksheet feels like something straight out of freshman year of high school, but if the homework theme makes you money, and I think it will, then who cares how silly it seems?

Step one is to learn in very precise terms how a company makes its money. Step two is to list and understand all the possible things that can affect the performance of the sector that the stock is in. "Sector" is another of those terms that can intimidate novice investors, but really it's pretty simple. Once you've done step one and figured out how a company makes its money, you know which sector, or industry group, the stock is in. Does the company make money by selling cars? It's in the auto sector. Does it make computers? That's technology. Does it sell health insurance? Then it straddles the insurance and health-care sectors and you'll have to do homework for both.

Step three is to examine the recent performance and behavior of both the stock and the company it represents a chunk of. Step four is to compare the stock to its competitors and make sure that its competitors don't represent a serious threat to its business. And finally, step five is to take a look at the company's income statement, balance sheet, and cash flow statement—but mostly the last two—to make sure that the company you are investing in is actually viable.

Now I'll tell you exactly how to do each step so that you can do your homework the way I do and with any luck make the kind of money I used to make at the hedge fund—or, and we're crossing our fingers here, do even better because you won't have to make all the mistakes I made over the years while developing this method.

Step one: to figure out how the company makes its money. This may sound obvious, and often it's the easiest thing in the world, but you have to do the due diligence anyway, because sometimes companies can fool you, and then you really get into trouble. You will need the annual report—that's the 10-K—which you can find in the section on SEC filings on most of the financial websites I cited above, or you can just go to the SEC's website and look up the company. The 10-Q—that's the quarterly report—is also worth looking at. I recommend looking over at least the last four quarters, but we're getting ahead of ourselves.

As I said, usually it's easy to figure out how a company makes its money. On my show I try not to recommend stocks that don't behave as advertised, but sometimes even I get taken in by a clever company. I'm good, but far from perfect. I like to use Boston Chicken, now known as Boston Market, and which is now owned by McDonald's, as an example of a company that didn't make its money the way you think it would. You would have thought that Boston Market was a fast-food place that made its money selling food to customers if you didn't do the homework. It's just intuitive, because Boston Chicken was a fast-food joint. But if you looked through their financials, through the annual and quarterly statements, you would have found that in fact, most of Boston Market's growth came from lending money to franchisees to get them off the ground and then gouging them. Long term, that was bad for business, and the company went bankrupt. What you thought was a restaurant was actually a poorly run bank. That's the value of homework.

More recently, you had Lucent (LU) making half its profits from interest on its pension fund. That's not really what you want in a stock. And then you could look at IMAX (IMX.TO) in 2004 and 2005. This was a company that consistently hit its earnings estimates, always a good thing on Wall Street, but not because people were going to IMAX movies. They were making their money by selling off parts of the company and getting deposits back on leases they were backing out of. That's a company making money off failure, not success, and it's not tenable over the long run. This is why we do our homework.

But let's say you're dealing with a high-quality company—and those are generally the kind I like to recommend—like Caterpillar (CAT) or Boeing (BA). These guys aren't complicated. Caterpillar sells big trucks and construction equipment, and Boeing sells airplanes. That's how they make their money. You still should make sure of this by looking at the financials, but when you look, you won't find any unpleasant surprises. I have to reiterate here that even if I'm super bullish on a stock, even if I hit the self-explanatory triple-buy button a dozen times and the bull button twice and throw in a gong button for good measure, you cannot, you *must not* own a stock unless you can explain to a friend who knows nothing about business precisely how the company behind that stock makes money. If you don't know how it makes money, you won't be able to understand anything else about the company, and that will ultimately leave you up the creek without a paddle. I dress up, drink and eat dopey foods, and, yes, wear diapers to show you and force you to remember how a company makes money.

Why else do we do homework? You need to know more than just how a company works before buying a chunk of it. You might know how a car operates, but that's not enough reason to buy one car over another, right? So step two of homework has you look at the performance of the sector the company is in and how the company stacks up against the competition in its sector. I know that some people hear words like "sector" and just want to hit the snooze button—something I should maybe add to the sound panel—but nothing is more important than the sector a stock lives in. Now, I will almost never, ever recommend a stock on *Mad Money* without giving you a pretty solid idea of the industry it's involved in. That would be just irresponsible, and I'm only irresponsible with my props on the show, never with your money. I've said this before on the show, and I'll say it again here in this book, because it's one of those facts that are just beyond important: half of what a stock does is totally dependent on its sector.

You'll know what sector your stock is in after you've done the homework to figure out how it makes its money, because sectors are just the part of the economy a company belongs to. If a company makes its money drilling for oil, then it's in the oil industry, and more broadly, the energy sector. There are lots of ways to slice and dice an economy, but you'll know how to look at the sector a company belongs to once you know where its money comes from.

If I get you interested in a stock, you should know what sector it's in, but it's worth taking a broader look at how that sector's been doing, and how it should do, because I can't give you a total rundown on how, say, the home builders operate in a ten-minute segment. If you read up on newspaper reports, if you take a look at the Wall Street research (which can be costly but is often worthwhile), if you look at the trade papers (these are industry-specific publications that are frequently overlooked, except on *Mad Money,* where I can't get enough of them, but that generally have great information), then you should be able to get a good handle on how a sector operates. And by that I mean what's good for the sector and what's bad for the sector.

Now on *Mad Money,* there are two kinds of good and bad when it comes to sectors, and it's helpful to distinguish between the two. There are events that help or hurt actual companies, and then there are stock-market-specific trading factors that help or hurt stocks. If you understand the difference between these two effects, you will understand my show and understand the market. If you look at the home builders, for example, the companies are hurt by higher interest rates. That's easy to understand: the higher interest rates go, the more expensive mortgages become, the fewer homes people buy, and the less money the home builders make.

When oil prices are high, everything in the oil patch does well in the market. Again, this is an example of an event that helps a company and raises its stock price. But what about these market factors, these Wall Street effects that mess with stock prices? Let's use another example. Whenever the Fed gets hawkish about raising rates, which tends to slow if not destroy the economy, or we get any other indicator that economic growth is going to be anemic, I'll come out and tell you to get defensive. People will often call defensive stocks "secular growth" stocks, and I use this term too, but that's unnecessary if authentic Wall Street gibberish. When I say "defense" I mean food and beverage companies, I mean drug companies; I'm talking about stocks that will keep delivering good earnings even in a bad economy. Coke and PepsiCo are both good examples of secular growth stocks you find in the supermarket; Johnson & Johnson is a great example of a secular growth stock you find in the pharmacy; and Procter & Gamble you find everywhere.

What do these guys have in common? A bad economy can't lay a hand on them. PepsiCo is going to grow earnings at 11 percent if we're in a good economy, and it'll grow earnings at 11 percent in a bad economy, and if you watch the show, you know that earnings growth is really what we're looking for in the vast majority of companies. But we don't need to get ahead of ourselves. What we're looking at are reasons that the stock market makes a company more or less valuable, even though nothing about the company changes. When the economy gets bad, PepsiCo doesn't do better, but the stock goes up—that's why I tell you to buy it. The stock goes up because big-time portfolio managers at hedge and mutual funds pull money out of companies that can't take the pain of a bad economy and pour it into ones that are much less affected by economic conditions. When economic growth picks up, PepsiCo might go down as these same investors take money out of it and send it back into the cyclical companies that kick butt in a strong economy.

Why did we go through all that? Because when you do your homework, you're really trying to understand the forces that make stocks move. If you don't know all the forces that act on a stock, you shouldn't own it, even if I tell you it's a great investment. You'll panic out the moment the stock gets hit.

The next two purposes of homework, steps three and four, are to check out performance, that's three, and competition, that's four. To check performance, just go through the newspaper articles and the quarterly filings to see if this is a stock that consistently lets the market down, or pleases the market, or doesn't do much either way. I don't like to recommend stocks that have been bad performers, but sometimes I'll pitch you a turnaround story, and in that case, you should try to get your head around why the company was doing badly before and why I think it'll do better in the future. In general, though,

I like to recommend performers and not companies with a history of disappointment.

Now when you do step four, when you check out the competition, you're really doing two things. You need to know if a company has any competitors—you'd be surprised at the number of monopolies just floating around—and if so, what kind of threat they pose to the business. The other part of checking out the competition, and usually the more important one, is to determine what a company is worth. The best way to do that is to stack it up against another company that does the same things.

For the benefit of the uninitiated, I'll take you through a quick tour of valuation here, because I talk about it a lot on the show, and I really don't want to leave anyone behind, especially because valuation is what lets you compare competitors. I know some of you are experts and don't need to hear about price to earnings ratios, but I want to bring even the English majors on board because everybody should be making money in the market.

Aside from speculative companies that don't make any profits, we value companies based on their earnings, their future expected earnings, and their growth. "Earnings" is just Wall Street's clumsy way of saying "profits." When you see a stock quote, that doesn't tell you a whole lot about valuation. What you want to look for is the stock's multiple, its price-to-earnings ratio, which you'll usually see expressed as P/E. This is simple arithmetic. Remember, we never do advanced math on *Mad Money*,—except sometimes behind the scenes. I think a fourth grader could make money in the market as long as she has a good grasp of division. The P/E multiple is a pretty simple thing: it's just the price of the stock divided by the earnings per share. It's how many times more than the earnings the market is willing to pay for the stock. If U.S. Steel (X) Earns $5.50 per share, and the stock trades at $67.50 (which is where it is as I write) then its P/E is 12.27. The price of a share of stock divided by the earnings per share. The P/E multiple is the real value of the stock versus other stocks for all intents and purposes. The multiple tells you what the market is willing to pay for the company's earnings, and it allows you to compare all stocks on an apples-to-apples basis. When you're looking at a company's competition, it should usually trade at about the same multiple as the company I've recommended. Companies in the same business trade together.

However, the real determinant of the multiple is the company's growth rate. You'll hear me say things on *Mad Money* about how I won't pay more than twice growth for a company. All that means is that if a company's earnings are growing at a 10 percent clip, I don't think you should pay more than 20 times earnings for it—a 20 multiple. When I've paid more than twice the growth rate I've lost too much money. By comparing growth rates and multiples, you can get a good picture of how a company is being valued against its competitors, and how it should be valued.

I should pause to point out something extremely important here. On *Mad Money,* as at my hedge fund, I don't care about the past; I care only about the future. When you look up a company's earnings on Yahoo! Finance, for example, you'll get the trailing-twelve-month earnings—in other words, last year's earnings. On the show, I almost always talk about forward earnings estimates, because really, I want to know where a stock is going in a year or two, not where it ought to be right now. The P/E you see on Yahoo! does have some value, but if you want to be on the same page as I am, and believe me, that's a good page to make money on, you should look at the forward earnings estimates, which you can find pretty easily. Most companies give an estimate of what they'll earn in the future, but it's more important to know what the Street is looking for than what the company is expecting. It's because traders and investors mostly care about what analysts, *not* companies, are saying. Analysts' estimates are loosely based on what companies tell them, though. For simplicity's sake, you can find those forward estimates if you click on the Analyst Estimates link on the left side of Yahoo! Finance or TheStreet.com, or anywhere else.

If you want to go farther into the future than the next fiscal year, you might have to pay for some Wall Street research, or if you're cheap, you could go hunting through newspaper articles and maybe you'll get lucky.

Multiples and earnings estimates and growth rates—all this stuff looks much more complicated and much harder to understand in the abstract than it does when we deal with a concrete example. If you felt like any of what you just read was complex, or a little over your head, then I guarantee you, working through an example where we value different companies in the same business will make it all as clear as day. The example for valuation that I just can't resist using is Google (GOOG). This is a stock I was totally right about all the way up, from the IPO at $80 a share in August 2004 to the peak at about 470 in January 2006, when I came as close as necessary to calling the top. I don't want to talk about Google because it lets me gloat; I do enough gloating on the show. Google is the most illustrative example out there if we're trying to get our heads around price-to-earnings ratios and their relationship to growth.

Google is great because it shows just how arbitrary the actual price of a stock is. As it was on its way up, journalists would write columns or talk on TV about how "expensive" the stock was, because the dollar amount its shares cost looked so high. People would call *Mad Money* asking about how expensive it was at $200 or $300 a share. The actual stock price means nothing without context. So let me give you the context and we'll go through the whole valuation game.

As I write this—and remember, this book is not a source of up-to-date information; that's what *Mad Money* is for—Google is expected to earn $9.42 per share in 2006, and $12.55 per share in 2007. Those are the analyst consensus estimates, which is just the average of every estimate from all the analysts who cover the stock. These numbers, as I told you, you can get right off Yahoo! Finance or TheStreet.com, just by clicking the Analyst Estimates links. So if the analysts are estimating that Google will earn $9.42 a share this year, then we can say that, with Google trading at $400, you're paying $400 for a company with $9.42 of earnings this year and $12.55 of earnings next year. If Google was going to earn 94¢ this year, and the stock cost $40, no one would call it expensive, but it would be valued exactly the same because it would have the same multiple.

I'm using the forward earnings estimates here just to make sure we're all on the same metaphorical page, because when you buy a share of Google, you're not paying for the earnings it made before you bought the stock; you're paying for the earnings it will make in the future. So if Google should earn $9.42 in 2006, and it costs $400, then you just divide the stock price by the earnings to get the price-to-earnings ratio, a.k.a. the P/E, the multiple, the real number that tells you the value of the stock. If you do the arithmetic—and you know there's no higher mathematics on *Mad Money* or in the Mad Money book, just arithmetic that a fourth grader could do—then you'll see that Google trades at 42 times expected 2006 earnings. It has a 42 multiple—that's its "real" value. Do the arithmetic again with the 2007 earnings estimate—$12.55 a share—and you'll see that Google trades at a little less than 32 times expected 2007 earnings when the share price is at $400, roughly one-times its growth rate! Dirt cheap!

The best thing about knowing these multiples is that this information lets you compare Google to other companies on the same basis, that is, in terms of valuation. Let's do a little comparison so that you understand what makes a good comparison and what makes a useless one. Google has a 42 multiple on its 2006 earnings estimates. Microsoft (MSFT), another big tech company, sits at a price of $22.86 a share as I write this, with estimated 2006 earnings of $1.26 per share—only an 18 multiple on this year's earnings. Your instincts should be telling you that Google is way more expensive than Microsoft. *But half of beating the market is beating your instincts.* Another 10 percent is listening to your instincts. You just have to know which ones to obey. As I said earlier, the thing that really determines a stock's multiple is its growth rate. Wall Street, and by Wall Street I mean all the big mutual funds and hedge funds that do most of the buying and selling, pays big money for growth, for earnings that are increasing quickly every year, and little for slow growth.

Microsoft's five-year expected annual growth rate is 12 percent— you get this number from the analyst estimates page just like all the rest. Google, over the next five years, is expected to grow its earnings at 31 percent every year. Google is growing a lot faster than Microsoft, and therefore it deserves a much higher multiple.

Now, let me give you another acronym: PEG, which is just your price-to-earnings multiple divided by the company's growth rate. On the Street we would say that Microsoft, with 12-percent growth and an 18 multiple, trades at 1.5 times growth. Google, with that 42 multiple and 31-percent growth, trades at just 1.35 times growth. So actually, even though Google is a $400 stock and Microsoft is a 23 stock, even though Google has a 42 multiple and Microsoft has an 18 multiple, Google is, by this very important measure called the PEG, cheaper than Microsoft.

As I said earlier, if a stock ever trades at two times growth or above, I consider it too expensive, and I think you should sell it. That's not because that's some magic number; it's because the growth-oriented mutual funds and hedge funds that manage most of the money in the market usually won't pay more than two times growth for a stock. And these guys, because they do most of the buying and selling, are the lawgivers. The market is a plutocracy: people with more money have more power in deciding what things are worth. They make these stocks too risky to own.

To get back to our example for a second, you want to compare companies in the same business with similar growth. Microsoft and Google have little in common so comparing them is just an example I used to show you how valuation is done. If you don't want to compare Google to Microsoft, compare it to Yahoo! (YHOO), which is in the same business: it makes its money from advertising on Internet searches, and it has a similar growth rate. Yahoo!'s estimated five-year growth rate is 28 percent. Its P/E based on the 2006 analyst consensus earnings estimate, which as I write this I believe is too low, is 63.5. Remember, Google has a 42 multiple on those 2006 estimates. Yahoo!'s 2006 PEG is 2.26, compared to Google's 1.35. This is a useful comparison, because Google and Yahoo! are both growing at close to the same rate, 31 percent and 28 percent, and they're both in the exact same business. This comparison, if the earnings estimates are right, tells you that Google is much cheaper than Yahoo! and probably undervalued. And that's what a legitimate, useful comparison that can actually make you money looks like. You don't have to use the five-year annual growth rate—I just used that for the example. I usually use next year's growth and next year's earnings estimates to make my calculations. Again, not because that's the objectively correct way to do things, but because that's how the big funds do it, and the big funds are the price setters, as I've just explained.

So to reiterate the whole of step four: you must check out the competition. First you're looking to see if the competition will hurt the stock you like. If it's Google you want to find research or newspaper articles talking about Google, Yahoo!, and Interactive Corp. (IACI) to make sure the other guys aren't eating into Google's market share. Then you want to use P/E multiples and growth rates to compare your stock (Google) to its competitors (like Yahoo!) and see if it's over- or undervalued relative to the competition.

There's one more step to doing homework, step five—you should never forget to look at a company's balance sheet and its cash-flow statement. I just hate companies with lots of debt, because bankruptcy will totally wipe out the value of the stock. Make sure the stock you're looking at has a healthy balance sheet, meaning either no debt or the cash to pay off its debt on time, before you move forward with one of my picks. If a stock has a bad balance sheet, it better have a good excuse. Usually, if I've recommended it on the show, I've given you the excuse because I really don't like to get behind companies with lots of debt.

Looking at balance sheets is another good place to use an example, because this stuff is much more interesting and much easier to grasp in practice than in principle. Google, to keep running with the same company, has a pristine balance sheet. It has no debt. It is also sitting on more than $8 billion of cash as I write this. Cash gives you flexibility. Debt, as anyone who's ever had a lot of personal debt knows, takes away that flexibility and just weighs you down.

But a lot of companies have debt. Caterpillar (CAT) has $25 billion debt, and it's not even a $50-billion company. But I'm not worried about CAT's debt, and you shouldn't be either. How can you know which debt to worry about and which debt is safe? By examining the company's balance sheet. Here is Caterpillar's balance sheet, right from Yahoo! Finance, where you can download it just as I did. Follow me. Be aware when you look at a balance sheet the all figures are in thousands, and that numbers in parentheses are negative.

Caterpillar's Balance Sheet for 2005, courtesy of Yahoo! Finance

PERIOD ENDING	12/31/05	12/31/04	12/31/03
Assets			
Current Assets			
Cash and Cash Equivalents	1,108,000	445,000	342,000
Short-Term Investments	—	—	—
Net Receivables	14,312,000	14,367,000	11,978,000
Inventory	5,224,000	4,675,000	3,047,000
Other Current Assets	2,146,000	1,369,000	1,424,000
Total Current Assets	22,790,000	20,856,000	16,791,000

Long-Term Investments	11,903,000	9,856,000	8,704,000
Property Plant and Equipment	7,988,000	7,682,000	7,290,000
Goodwill	1,451,000	1,450,000	1,398,000
Intangible Assets	424,000	315,000	239,000
Accumulated Amortization	—	—	—
Other Assets	1,745,000	2,258,000	1,427,000
Deferred Long-Term Asset Charges	768,000	674,000	616,000
Total Assets	**47,069,000**	**43,091,000**	**36,465,000**
Liabilities			
Current Liabilities			
Accounts Payable	9,024,000	8,522,000	6,883,000
Short-/Current Long-Term Debt	10,068,000	7,688,000	5,738,000
Other Current Liabilities	—	—	—
Total Current Liabilities	**19,092,000**	**16,210,000**	**12,621,000**
Long-Term Debt	15,677,000	15,837,000	14,078,000
Other Liabilities	2,991,000	2,986,000	3,172,000
Deferred Long-Term Liability Charges	877,000	591,000	516,000
Minority Interest	—	—	—
Negative Goodwill	—	—	—
Total Liabilities	**38,637,000**	**35,624,000**	**30,387,000**
Stockholders' Equity			
Misc. Stocks Options Warrants	—	—	—
Redeemable Preferred Stock	—	—	—
Preferred Stock	—	—	—
Common Stock	1,859,000	1,231,000	1,059,000
Retained Earnings	11,808,000	9,937,000	8,450,000
Treasury Stock	(4,637,000)	(3,277,000)	(2,914,000)
Capital Surplus	—	—	—
Other Stockholder Equity	(596,000)	(424,000)	(517,000)
Total Stockholder Equity	**8,432,000**	**7,467,000**	**6,078,000**
Net Tangible Assets	**$6,557,000**	**$5,702,000**	**$4,441,000**

Look at the balance sheet under "Current Liabilities" and find the line that says "Short-/Current Long-Term Debt." That's a combination of short-term debt and long-term debt that's coming due soon. Then go to the cash-flow statement—this thing is really simple, concrete, and great: it just documents where a company spends its money and where it gets its money. On an income statement you have all kinds of abstract things like tax credits or amortization that don't represent any money changing hands. But the cash-flow statement just tells you about the money that's changing hands. I'm including this, too, so that you can follow along.

Caterpillar's Cash-Flow Statement for 2005, courtesy of Yahoo! Finance

PERIOD ENDING	12/31/05	12/31/04	12/31/03
Net Income	2,854,000	2,035,000	1,099,000
Operating Activities, Cash Flows Provided by or Used In			
Depreciation	1,477,000	1,397,000	1,347,000
Adjustments to Net Income	(20,000)	(113,000)	(15,000)
Changes in Accounts Receivable	(908,000)	(7,616,000)	(521,000)
Changes in Liabilities	1,144,000	1,457,000	617,000
Changes in Inventories	(568,000)	(1,391,000)	(286,000)
Changes in Other Operating Activities	(866,000)	240,000	(175,000)
Total Cash Flow from Operating Activities	3,113,000	(3,991,000)	2,066,000
Investing Activities, Cash Flows Provided by or Used In			
Capital Expenditures	(2,415,000)	(2,114,000)	(1,765,000)
Investments	(2,471,000)	3,708,000	(1,504,000)
Other Cash Flows from Investing Activities	1,361,000	483,000	708,000
Total Cash Flows from Investing Activities	(3,525,000)	2,077,000	(2,561,000)

Financing Activities, Cash Flows Provided by or Used In			
Dividends Paid	(618,000)	(534,000)	(491,000)
Sale Purchase of Stock	(1,202,000)	(222,000)	(248,000)
Net Borrowings	2,973,000	2,630,000	1,252,000
Other Cash Flows from Financing Activities	—	—	—
Total Cash Flows from Financing Activities	1,153,000	1,874,000	513,000
Effect of Exchange Rate Changes	(78,000)	143,000	15,000
Change in Cash and Cash Equivalents	$663,000	$103,000	$33,000

On this statement, you can see how much actual money a company makes from its operations, its business, its investments, and how much money goes to repay debt or gets borrowed. To figure out if a company is in control of its debt, first see if it's borrowing or paying off debt on the cash-flow statement. With the most recent data you are looking at right now, Caterpillar is borrowing money, not paying off debt. Ordinarily that's not good, but in this case that doesn't bother me, but only because of the context. CAT is a profitable company that generates enough cash to take care of its debts, and it's borrowing money to grow its operations. You can tell that CAT can pay its debts on time by looking at the cash-flow statement and seeing that even though, as of the end of 2005, it had $10 billion of debt due in 2006, which you can see on the balance sheet below liabilities, next to short-/current long-term debt, an amount three times the size of its operating cash flow, it is in a position to refinance and ultimately pay off that debt. If you look at the "Financing Activities" section of the cash-flow statement, you'll see that people are still willing to loan Caterpillar money. Since Caterpillar's assets on the balance sheet are much greater than its liabilities—$47 billion in assets compared to $38.6 billion in liabilities—it won't have financing problems.

If you want to see what a bad balance sheet looks like, just look at Calpine's from the end of 2005. Calpine was a failed energy company. Here's why it failed:

Calpine's Balance Sheet for 2005, courtesy of Yahoo! Finance

PERIOD ENDING	12/31/05	12/31/04	12/31/03
Assets			
Current Assets			
Cash and Cash Equivalents	1,677,510	1,829,164	1,760,942
Short-Term Investments	489,499	324,206	496,967
Net Receivables	1,025,886	1,097,157	988,947
Inventory	189,986	179,395	140,305
Other Current Assets	45,156	133,643	89,593
Total Current Assets	**3,428,037**	**3,563,565**	**3,476,754**
Long-Term Investments	962,970	709,730	1,360,357
Property Plant and Equipment	14,119,215	21,160,605	20,193,200
Goodwill	45,160	45,160	45,160
Intangible Assets	78,375	73,190	229,877
Accumulated Amortization	—	—	—
Other Assets	1,700,231	1,241,232	1,597,852
Deferred Long-Term Asset Charges	210,809	422,606	400,732
Total Assets	**20,544,797**	**27,216,088**	**27,303,932**
Liabilities			
Current Liabilities			
Accounts Payable	723,966	1,571,821	1,374,539
Short-/Current Long-Term Debt	5,413,937	928,714	805,816
Other Current Liabilities	1,004,489	784,857	335,048
Total Current Liabilities	**7,142,412**	**3,285,392**	**2,515,403**
Long-Term Debt	2,462,462	11,358,381	18,020,269
Other Liabilities	15,680,585	6,455,256	259,551
Deferred Long-Term Liability Charges	492,039	1,135,941	1,476,564
Minority Interest	275,384	393,445	410,892
Negative Goodwill	—	—	—
Total Liabilities	**26,052,882**	**22,628,415**	**22,682,679**

Stockholders' Equity			
Misc. Stocks Options Warrants	—	—	—
Redeemable Preferred Stock	—	—	—
Preferred Stock	—	—	—
Common Stock	569	537	415
Retained Earnings	(8,613,160)	1,326,048	1,588,509
Treasury Stock	—	—	—
Capital Surplus	3,265,458	3,151,577	2,995,735
Other Stockholder Equity	(160,952)	109,511	56,594
Total Stockholder Equity	**(5,508,085)**	**4,587,673**	**4,621,253**
Net Tangible Assets	**($5,631,620)**	**$4,469,323**	**$4,346,216**

Let me give you a few highlights that should, if you see them elsewhere, raise some serious red flags. As of December 31, 2005, Calpine's liabilities exceeded its assets by $6 billion, or about 30 percent. So the company was in the hole for more than it was actually worth. It had current liabilities, mostly short-term debt and long-term debt that had come due, of more than $7 billion. Current liabilities are the bills a company has to pay in the next twelve months. Since its liabilities were greater than its assets, Calpine wasn't in a position to get good financing because lending it money was clearly a bad investment. When you see that a company has $7 billion of bills to pay, you'd better run to the cash-flow statement to see if it can generate that money.

Calpine's Cash-Flow Statement for 2005, courtesy of Yahoo! Finance

PERIOD ENDING	12/31/05	12/31/04	12/31/03
Net Income	(9,939,208)	(242,461)	282,022
Operating Activities, Cash Flows Provided by or Used In			
Depreciation	760,023	833,375	735,341

Adjustments to Net Income	8,802,803	(443,405)	(116,964)
Changes in Accounts Receivable	(42,437)	(99,447)	(221,243)
Changes in Liabilities	(170,554)	176,322	(84,271)
Changes in Inventories	—	—	—
Changes in Other Operating Activities	(100,360)	(214,489)	(304,326)
Total Cash Flow from Operating Activities	**(689,733)**	**9,895**	**290,559**
Investing Activities, Cash Flows Provided by or Used in			
Capital Expenditures	(773,988)	(1,545,480)	(1,886,013)
Investments	272,935	104,198	(32,817)
Other Cash Flows from Investing Activities	1,418,510	1,039,856	(596,535)
Total Cash Flows from Investing Activities	**917,457**	**(401,426)**	**(2,515,365)**
Financing Activities, Cash Flows Provided by or Used in			
Dividends Paid	—	—	—
Sale Purchase of Stock	4	360,098	175,678
Net Borrowings	(366,261)	(161,294)	2,437,495
Other Cash Flows from Financing Activities	206,328	(31,752)	10,813
Total Cash Flows from Financing Activities	**(159,929)**	**167,052**	**2,623,986**
Effect of Exchange Rate Changes	**(181)**	**16,101**	**13,140**
Change in Cash and Cash Equivalents	**$67,614**	**($208,378)**	**$412,320**

This is where things get ugly in this example. Calpine had negative cash flow from operations, which means its business was losing cash. It was in the hole there for a little less than $700 million. But maybe its cash flow from investments could save it? Well, in 2005, Calpine was up a little over $900 million from investments. That leaves it positive by about $219 million—still way below the $7 billion of bills to pay. Then you go to the financing section of the cash-flow statement and man, it gets worse. The company had to pay off some bills in 2005, which left it down almost $160 million. At the very bottom of our tour through Calpine's cash-flow statement, you can see the total cash that it generated in 2005: just over $67 million.

When a company's liabilities are greater than its assets, get out. If you really want to take a risk in a stock like Calpine, you can look at how much money it's going to owe in the next year—in this case in 2006, when it would have to pony up $7 billion. Then there's only one question: can the company pay? You go to the cash-flow statement and see that last year the company could only generate $67 million of cash, and you know it can't. Calpine would have to come up with a hundred times that amount just to pay the bills. It would take a miracle for a company to somehow pull off a 10,000-percent increase in cash generation in the course of a year. So when you see these things, you know a company is either financially too ugly to own or, even worse, destined for bankruptcy, which means the stock is going to zero. That's why we have step five: you always have to check out the balance sheet for red flags so you don't end up owning a real dog of a company.

That's your preliminary homework. Step one: figure out how a company makes money; step two: learn what types of things affect the performance of its sector; step three: find out about the company's past performance; step four: look at the competition for potential threats and, more important, so you can figure out a good valuation for the stock; and finally; step five: pay attention to that balance sheet and cash-flow statement.

Once you've gone through that homework, once you've learned all of that, you still should do one more thing. On *Mad Money*, if I tell you to buy a stock, I tell you why I think it will go up. I've got a good track record, but I'm not always right. So please, before you leap all over a Cramer stock, check out my thesis against the research and the journalism and whatever else might be pertinent to the argument. I don't make many factual mistakes on the show, but sometimes I'll tell you to buy a stock and I'll be wrong—let's take Dick's Sporting Goods (DKS) for a horribly painful example. I said this company had great regional-to-national growth right before it announced its quarterly earnings in August 2005, and it turned out I was wrong. If I'd done a little more homework, as I'm encouraging you to do, then I would have found out that they were going to disappoint because of a botched acquisition, something that was knowable from articles about the company, and I would have been a lot less bullish. Dick's got wiped out after that quarter, and even though ten months later, in May 2006, it was up above where I recommended it, I still consider my call a massive mistake. You've got to check my argument to make sure you agree with it before you buy.

And that, my friends, is the homework. Once you've done the homework and you're satisfied with the company, you've got the green light from Cramer to buy the stock. But I have to warn you, I'm very picky about how you're allowed to purchase stocks. And I'm picky for a reason: if you don't follow the rules, if you stray from the method, the odds are good you'll lose money.

3

BUYING A STOCK MAD MONEY STYLE

Step Three: Use Limit Orders and Buy Incrementally

Now it's time to buy, buy, buy. Give yourself a big, stuttering booyah, my favorite type of booyah. I'll go over what that extra weekly hour of maintenance homework is after I tell you how to buy the stock. We're doing this chronologically. First you do your research homework, then you buy the stock the right way, then you check up on it the right way, and then you sell it. (I'll cover that in the next chapter.)

There's a certain way I want you to go about buying stocks, especially the ones I recommend on *Mad Money*, because I feel a special responsibility to you for those, but my advice on buying stocks applies generally as well. Before I give you the procedure, I want you to take one more pause just so we all understand the context in which you buy a stock. Let's say you've got $10,000 of mad money—that's the money you can use to invest in stocks. That's not retirement money, which you probably want in a 401K or an IRA, a savings account, bonds, or only the most conservative of dividend-paying stocks. We've got this $10,000 portfolio. Now let's say you're going to own five stocks—that's the minimum you can own and still be diversified. You watch the show, so you know what it means to be diversified: no more than 20 percent of your portfolio is in any one sector. It means you're keeping your eggs in at least five separate baskets so at least some of them will hatch, no matter what happens.

If you're going to buy one stock I'm recommending—let's make it Boeing (BA), a big, strong aerospace name, just for the sake of this example—then you better not throw all your moolah into it. You better stay diversified. That means, of this imaginary ten grand, you put no more than two grand into Boeing. I don't care if you believe that Boeing will be the only stock that goes up ever again, you're only allowed to put 20 percent of your money into it. If you want to buy Cramer's stocks, then you'd better play by Cramer's rules. (Like on the show, I slip into the third person when I get extra serious, OK?) The rules aren't there to constrain you. They're there—and you can look them up in a later chapter in this book—because every time I've broken them I've lost money. Rather than having you make all my mistakes again, I'd rather you just take this advice in good faith and spare yourself the hurt.

And listen, let's say I just did a segment on all the parts that go into an airplane, because aerospace is strong—I've done this before, and it's not unlikely I'll do it again. Let's say you're so sold on every single aerospace stock I name in the segment that you want to own Boeing (BA), the company that makes the planes; Parker Hannifin (PH), which makes parts for planes; Aviall (AVL), which does outsourced maintenance work for airlines; Honeywell (HON), which also makes airplane parts, although Honeywell is a very diversified company; and Rolls-Royce (RR.L) for their magnificent airplane engines—engines, which, by the way, helped win World War II. That's an enormous no-no. Pick *one*. The aerospace cycle is great, but diversification is of paramount importance.

If you're buying Boeing (BA), you're buying it in the context of owning four other stocks in your $10,000 portfolio, with no one stock representing more than 20 percent of that money. Not one of those other four stocks should overlap. Give yourself a bank, let's say Bank of America (BAC) or Citigroup (C), and then maybe a retailer like a Nordstrom (JWN), a tech company like Qualcomm (QCOM), and maybe round it off with an oil-service name like Halliburton (HAL). There is no overlap in this portfolio, and if we were playing "Am I diversified?" I'd bless it. Now be careful. I'm writing this book well before it's published, and certainly well before you read it, so don't think that I want you to buy any of these names now. They're just examples. I'll give you up-to-date advice on *Mad Money*.

We've cleared the diversification hurdle, and now, finally, I know it's been killing you to wait so long, you can start buying some Boeing. But we're gonna take it real slow, not because I don't have faith in your abilities, but because that's how the pros do it, and I want to turn you into a pro. We've gone through a whole pipeline to get here. I recommend Boeing on the show because I think we've got at least three more years of strong airplane orders. You've decided that Boeing is a low-risk name you're comfortable owning, then you did all your homework, as just explained, and finally, you've made sure there's a place for it in your diversified portfolio.

Let's start buying. You want to buy $2,000 of Boeing, but you don't want to do it all at once. Trust me—this is rule number three from my Twenty-Five Investment Rules to Live By in *Jim Cramer's Real Money*. If you buy all at once, you'll more often than not end up hating yourself. The same is true of selling all at once, because stocks are volatile.

Let's say you buy all $2,000 worth of BA and then the next day the stock is down a dollar. You'll feel like a total moron. On *Mad Money*, we build positions incrementally. You don't have to buy the stock one share at a time, but since commissions are so low, let's say you do it in four installments.

If you can, try to wait for some weakness in the stock and buy it on a dip. We can't always buy low and sell high—sometimes we have to buy high and sell higher—but patience is generally a virtue when it comes to buying stocks. Boeing is a big company, so it won't go up much if I recommend it on the show, but the twenty-four-hour rule is still in effect. I'd look for any weakness in the stock—that is, any time the stock comes down—in the next week after the day I recommend it, to start buying, although I often try to wait until a down day to recommend a stock. If you don't get weakness, then don't wait forever. After a week or two, patience can start to become a vice. After five or six days, if you don't see any weakness, pull the trigger anyway and buy $500 of the stock.

Oh, there's that awful word again: "buy." When you play with Cramer, you don't buy stock. Buying stock means using a market order, and market orders are, as far as I'm concerned, gilded, handwritten invitations to your stockbroker to rip you off. A market order lets your broker offer anything for a stock you're trying to buy or sell; it's easily conceivable that if you just say "buy," you could end up paying 1 or 2 percent above the asking price (the price that someone's offering to sell the stock for) just because there's nobody looking out for you.

That's why I always tell you to use limit orders. I hope you're listening. So you call up your broker, or you hit up the brokerage Web site, since this is the twenty-first century, and you place a limit order for six shares of BA, assuming that Boeing is trading at roughly $83.33, not far from where it is as I write this. That should work out to about $500. When you place a limit order, you get to set a cap on how much you're willing to pay per share, and it doesn't cost you a dime extra to do this. It's like free money. You can set your own price; you can be stingy or generous. Sometimes if your limit is too low, you won't get the stock, but at least you're not being ripped off. I'd say in general, you're doing yourself a disservice if you're setting your limit more than 0.15 percentage points above the last bid, the last offer someone's made for the stock. And also, I should add, when you place a limit, you can either set it to expire at the end of the trading day or let it go on until you cancel it. Please, I beg you, just to be careful, always choose to have your limit order expire at the end of the trading day. If you can't fill it then, just set another limit order the next morning. You don't want some nasty surprise where you set a limit order to buy a share of Boeing for $83.43—that is, no higher than that price—and then overnight Boeing reports something awful, the stock plummets to 70, and you end up paying $80 for it the next morning just because you didn't choose to have your limit order expire at the end of the day.

With a big stock like Boeing, you can use a really tight limit, and you should be able to get those six hypothetical shares for $500. Let's walk this example all the way through. To buy that Boeing you call your broker, or you go online and use one of the discount Internet brokers, and you either tell your broker or the computer screen that you want to buy six shares of Boeing (BA) for no more than $83.40 per share, if the last trade was $83.33. Your broker should be able to fill that limit, even though it's very tight, which means it's very close to the last trade, because Boeing is a large-cap name without a lot of volatility. (You can use an electronic firm; because you and I have done the work together without a stockbroker, we don't need to pay higher fees.)

But suppose a couple of hours go by and your broker just can't fill that limit order. You still want the stock, but you don't want to feel like you're chasing it. You can get more generous with your limit. First cancel the last limit order, and then put in a new one. Let's say the last trade of Boeing was at $83.45, which is above your previous limit, which is why you couldn't fill the limit. Now to get the stock, tell your broker or your electronic broker that you want to buy six shares of Boeing at $83.60 per share. That's 15¢ above the last trade. Unless there's some serious momentum driving Boeing up, your broker should be able to fill that limit order. Now you've got six shares of Boeing.

What's next? Building a position takes time. Keep waiting for weakness in Boeing, not just over the next day, but also over the next several days—even weeks. If you feel like the stock is really going to ramp, then I sanction pulling the trigger and building your position much more quickly, because you don't want to miss making that money. But in general, I'm always in favor of waiting around, at least for a little while, for some weakness. And always, always use those limit orders. (You already have some stock on, so the worse that happens is it goes higher.)

Now once you've got yourself a core position set up in Boeing, or any other stock I recommend on the show—we can talk later about trading around that position and selling it—but once you've executed this kind of buy, and done this kind of homework, give yourself a pat on the back, because you're doing exactly what I would do, and you are way, way ahead of the game.

But you'll only stay ahead of the game if you keep up your homework. You've got to do one hour a week of homework on Boeing, because in my book, and this *is* my book, if you don't spend an hour a week studying up on each stock you own, you're setting yourself up for failure. Remember, my mantra is buy and homework, not buy and hold. You've already done the preliminary homework before buying the stock, so you should be familiar with all the tools we use to do homework on the Internet.

So what are you looking at in your weekly homework? First of all, you should check the share price every day, at least once. You don't have to fanatically monitor the price every five minutes like a madman if you're not trading (I'll address trading later in the book), but you should be aware of where your stock is trading on any given day, and since this barely takes two seconds, I don't even count it as part of the homework. Besides, if the stock is up, even just a little, you'll feel so good you won't think of it as homework either. Your follow-up, maintenance homework is really about making sure that all the things that were true when you bought and liked the stock stay true.

Let me give you a list of things that, no matter the stock, you have to watch out for in your weekly homework. And I'll do this in steps, too. Step one of your maintenance homework is to make sure the earnings are OK. You need to watch and see if the company revises its own earnings forecasts, or if the analysts who cover it change their forecasts. This can be a good thing or a bad thing; either way, it's the most important thing for you to keep an eye on. Step two is to make sure that your reason for owning a stock, the thesis that I lay out on my show, is still true. With Boeing the thesis was that we're in the middle of a seven-year-long aerospace cycle where all the airlines are replacing their jets and, in addition, that Airbus, Boeing's only serious competitor, was failing miserably to keep up. With different companies the thesis will be different, but as long as you read all the relevant newspaper articles about the stock or the story it's a part of, you should have an easy time keeping a handle on the continued relevance of the big thesis. If you feel really lost, you can always pony up some money for some Wall Street research, although I don't like that. Please feel free to call into *Mad Money,* or *RealMoney,* my radio show, to ask me if I still agree with the thesis. Remember, I take callers and I'm here to help. Calling *Mad Money* can absolutely be a part of your homework. Step three is a catchall. Remember, step two of your initial homework was figuring out what forces move the stock. Step three of your maintenance homework is watching those forces—again, you can probably find whatever information you need in the newspaper or on the Internet. I can't tell you precisely what to look for because, contrary to my own sometimes inflated self-opinion, I don't know the future, and there are unexpected events that will move your stock that I can't predict. Part of step three is watching to see if anything new pops up on the horizon that will mess with or help out your stock. The price of wealth is eternal vigilance.

I'm making it sound like you're only watching out for bad news when you do your hour a week of maintenance homework. And that's true: what you're really looking for is bad news, so that, if it turns out the stock won't make you money the way you thought it would, you can cut your losses and get out before losing too much money. That doesn't mean there won't be good news, and it doesn't mean you shouldn't pay attention to the good news. If you own a stock and it revises its earnings estimates up and the stock goes up big, you need to pay attention to that too. When good news happens to stocks you own, you should even celebrate because you just made money, and even though money can't buy happiness, making money always makes me happy. Good news can change the picture as much as bad news, but you don't need me to tell you to listen to the good news about your stocks. You don't need me to tell you to celebrate when your stocks go up. The good news pays for itself. It's the negative part of your homework that you really need to force yourself to do, because it's not as fun, and because it's so much more important.

If you own a stock that gets one piece of good news after another, you don't need to work very hard to make money—that stock is going up. In the next chapter, I'll tell you how to sell stocks that go up so you can take your money to the bank. But if you own a stock that gets hit with bad news, you've got some serious decisions to make. You could potentially lose a lot of money. Or the bad news could be a buying opportunity. You can't know which until you do your maintenance homework and integrate the new information with what you already know.

Now you know how to sift through my recommendations on *Mad Money* for the stocks that are right for you. You know how to do your homework on those stocks and find out everything you need to know before you buy them. You know how to buy stocks the right way, using limit orders and building a position gradually over time. And you also know how to do your hour a week of homework to check on your investments.

It's time for you to learn how to sell.

4

SELLING STOCKS
THE RIGHT WAY

You haven't made a dime in a stock until you sell it and take your profits to the bank. That's my Sixth Commandment of Trading from *Jim Cramer's Real Money.* You might own a stock that's doubled since you bought it, but you can't honestly say you've made money in that stock until you sell the stock and cash out. I told you how I want you to research the stocks I pick on *Mad Money,* and I told you how you should buy them if you want to try to get rich. But if I'm going to do my job responsibly, I also have to tell you how to sell. Remember, my goal in this part of the book is to take you step by step from one of my picks on *Mad Money* to a big cash deposit in your bank of choice. You've bought the stock and you know how to do the maintenance homework, but until you sell, you're not all the way there.

But before we can talk about *how* to sell, we should go over *why* you're selling in the first place. There are two good reasons to sell a stock: because it's made you money or because it's going to lose you money. On *Mad Money,* I don't devote nearly as much time to selling as I do to buying stocks because selling is much more subjective. I know a lot of people feel like they've been left out on their own and betrayed when I come out and tell them to sell a stock on the "Lightning Round" even though I recommended it as a buy in a longer segment two months before. A lot of people think that's flip-flopping. They think it's inconsistent and just shows that I'm an idiot. Maybe I'm an idiot, but not about this. The market is dynamic. Things change. That's why you do your homework, to monitor those changes. And sometimes, for positive or negative reasons, a stock that was a buy becomes a sell. Now, one thing is for sure, you absolutely cannot wait for me to tell you to sell a stock on *Mad Money* before you pull the trigger and sell it yourself. Selling is almost a personal decision; it's one you must make on your own if you want to make money instead of losing it by waiting for permission from me to sell a stock. It is why I developed the Thursday night sell block, but it's still not enough.

But I would feel terrible about leaving you on your own to sell the stocks I've recommended without telling you how to do it. As I said before, there are two good reasons to sell: you're either taking profits or you're cutting losses. People have serious trouble with both of these concepts because they get caught up in the emotion of owning a stock. Owning stocks should be fun; that's my mantra. But you can't become attached to a single stock for irrational reasons. We have fun because investing is interesting and, more important, I hope because we're making truckloads of money. We don't have fun because stocks we love go up. Stocks are just pieces of paper; you're not allowed to love them. You can't have emotional attachments to stocks. If a stock you bought at $50 goes down to $20 because the company's fundamentals have deteriorated beyond repair, you can't keep hanging on, waiting to sell until the stock gets back to $50 so that you haven't lost money on the investment. That's irrational. Cut your losses, sell the stock at $20 take the pain, and buy a stock that's going up.

And by the same token, if a stock you bought at $50 goes up to $80, then sell some of it—sell most of it. I know you get attached to the stock. I know it feels good to own a stock that's made you a 60 percent gain. But it hasn't actually made you anything until you sell it. Even if you have total confidence that the stock is going even higher, you can't make money until you sell. You're a pig if you don't sell. You don't have to sell everything. Remember, I told you how to buy incrementally; you should also sell incrementally when you're taking profits. You can still own some of that great stock that's made you a bunch of money, but you should sell a lot of it to lock in your profits.

This leads us to the two big questions: how do you know when it's time to cut your losses and how do you know when it's time to take profits? I'll address these separately. I start with profit taking because if you're taking my advice on the show, doing your homework, and buying stocks the smart way, you should be taking profits more often than you have to cut your losses.

Taking Profits the Right Way

I always like to say that it doesn't matter where a stock's come from, all that matters is where that stock is going. That's only half true. When it comes to cutting your losses, to selling a bad stock that's gone down, then it doesn't matter where you bought it, only where it's going. But when we're talking about selling a stock that's gone up, a stock that's making you money, then it absolutely matters where that stock has come from. Let's say you bought Sears Holdings (SHLD) at $100, and now it's at $150. Now let's say someone else bought Sears at $140 and it's still at $150. Both of you believe Sears will go higher, but are you both in the same position?

Absolutely not. The guy who bought Sears at $100 has a 50 percent gain. That's an enormous win. He should take a lot of that off the table. Even if you think Sears is going higher, if you have a 50 percent gain, I'd recommend selling, at minimum, a third of your stock. Honestly, you should probably sell half or even more, just to lock in those big profits. I'll give you some hard and fast rules for profit taking in a minute, I just want to use this example to give you a sense of how subjective profit taking can be.

Let's go back to that guy who bought Sears at $140. With the stock up 10 points since then, he's got a cool 7 percent gain. Seven percent is good, but if you believe Sears is going higher, then you probably don't want to sell much stock when it's up 7 percent. It depends on how much of a trader you are. If you don't like making a lot of trades, then I wouldn't take any off the table. But if you want to lock in a little of that money, you might take just 10 percent off the table. The point here is that the situation is totally different depending on how much profit you have. Profit taking in a good stock is subjective.

Notice, the whole time I went through this example, I stressed the fact that both of these investors believe that Sears is going up. If you think Sears is coming down, that's a totally different story. That's a question of cutting your losses, and I'll get to that later. Right now we're just dealing with a situation in which a stock you own has gone up and you think it's going higher. Truth be told, this whole game requires flexibility, and you shouldn't adhere strictly to any tight rules about profit taking. I can't tell you to sell a quarter of your position when the stock goes up by some percentage amount. How much you take off the table depends on two things: how big your gain in is the stock, which we already went over, and how much higher you think it can go. I'll help out on the show, and you can always call in and ask me on the "Lightning Round", where I think the stock is going, but you should have your own opinion. You'll get that from doing homework.

Even though I want to, I can't give you a strict set of rules that will regulate when you should take profits. But I can give you a set of guidelines that, as long as you follow them, should help you take profits in the best way possible. Here are six guidelines that you should follow when trying to take profits in a healthy stock, a stock you think is going higher. First, one great rule of thumb is that you should try to keep your position the same size as the stock increases in value. By size, I mean the monetary value of the position. So if you own $2,000 of Boeing, as we talked about in the last chapter, and then the stock goes up 10 percent, you'll own $2,200 worth of Boeing stock. When that happens, you can "trim"—that's Wall Street/gardening gibberish—your position. You wanted a $2,000 position in Boeing, and you got there by buying twenty-four shares at about $83 a share. Now Boeing is at about $91, so if you sell two shares, you'll trim your position back to $2,018—much closer to the size of your original position.

Keeping your position roughly the same size as a stock increases in value is a good general rule to follow. It will always keep you from becoming a pig, and that's essential. But that rule alone is not enough. I don't want you to sell a tiny little bit when a stock is up 2 percent; unless you're day-trading, that's not a gain worth taking. As I've been saying, selling stocks correctly is subjective. That's why it's so hard for me to tell you personally when to sell. But the rest of my guidelines will stop you from being a pig, and that's the important thing.

Guideline number two—remember, these aren't rules—is that you should set a target price for where you think a stock is going. What's a target price? It's the price you think the stock is headed to. It's not the top; ideally, it will be below the top. A lot of people want to sell stocks at the top, when they're at their very highest, but that's a dangerous game. It's like playing chicken, because a top means that a stock is about to come down. I'd rather have you taking your profits while a stock is on the way up than have you watch your profits erode as you take them on the way down. Now how do you set a target price? If I recommend a stock on the show, I'll usually give you a rough idea of where I think the stock is headed. Your target price will be based on a lot of things, but primarily it should be based on comparing P/E and PEG rate multiples with a company's peer group—the other stocks that look like it. The stock might be undervalued based on its growth rate and earnings compared to its peers when you buy it, so you'll use where its peers trade to set your target price. Or you might buy a stock because you think its earnings estimates are going to be revised upward. For example, if you buy a stock with a P/E of 10 and expected earnings of a dollar a share, that stock trades at $10. But if you think that those earnings estimates will be revised up to $1.50 a share, if that's the thesis behind owning the stock, then your price target should be $15, because after the revision, the stock will keep the same multiple, but it will have higher expected earnings. How do you get this thesis? If it's a stock I'm telling you to buy on the show, then you can get it straight from me. Otherwise, when you do your homework properly, once you figure out what a company does to make money, and then you figure out what forces act on the stock and its sector, you should have a good idea of where the stock will go.

Earlier I said that traditionally we define peers as companies that are in the same business, but I'm not a traditional kind of guy. You don't want to limit your evaluation to companies in the same business or even companies in the same sector. It's imperative that you know what the market will pay for growth. What's that mean? At different times, depending on the state of the economy and other big trends, the market will value growth differently. Once again, when I say "the market," I'm really just talking about the handful of mutual funds and hedge funds that do most of the investing and all think the same way. Pretty much everybody who runs money got into the business through the same few investment banks, so they've all been taught to think the same way. Ultimately, since these guys are the buyers and the sellers, they set prices. If you're setting a price target for a stock you own, you want to know what they will pay for that stock's earnings growth. And to do that you don't just look at a company's traditional peers. You have to look at other companies with similar growth rates in other industries. Let's say you own a stock with 15 percent earnings growth. If you're going to set a price target, you need to know what kind of multiple the market is generally paying for that 15 percent growth. So find a bunch of other companies with 14, 15, or 16 percent growth and see what their P/E multiples are. That'll tell you what the market is willing to pay for stocks with similar growth at any given moment, and that should be another big factor in setting your price target. If the market's willing to pay twenty times earnings for 15 percent growth, that's a 20 P/E and a PEG of 1.33. You probably shouldn't expect your 15 percent growth stock to get much more than a 20 multiple.

So you have a price target for your stock. Let's keep using Boeing, which we bought last chapter at $83.33. Let's say our price target for Boeing is $100. What do we do with that target? That's guideline number three: when a stock reaches your price target, unless you get new information that causes you to move that target up, you shouldn't think the stock is going much higher. This one's pretty intuitive. When Boeing hits $100, your price target for the stock, you no longer believe that Boeing is going higher. It might flatline, it might go lower, but the point is that once you hit the target, you're not positive on the stock anymore. So what do you do?

Guideline number four: when you stop thinking—not believing, thinking—that a stock you own will go higher, you sell it. You don't have to dump it all at once; in fact, that's foolish. You should still be selling incrementally, even though this is a bigger decision than regular profit taking. Selling incrementally is a discipline you never break. However, you'll want to sell faster after your stock hits its price target and you no longer think it has much juice left in it. There's no reason for you to own a stock if you don't think it's going up. And hanging on past your price target is investing on the basis of hope, or it's buy and hold, and both of those are surefire ways to lose money.

But let's say you've got your hands on a really great stock that keeps revising upward its earnings estimates and growth estimates, a stock that's totally on fire, where you consistently move your price target up because there's so much positive new information about the company. When do you clear out of a stock like that, where the upside seems hard to quantify because the company just keeps delivering? Well, first, refer to guideline number one: trim your position so that you never own more of a company, in terms of a dollar amount, than you want to. If the stock keeps going up, keep trimming. If Boeing does so well that the only reasonable price target is 160, almost double what you paid for it in the last chapter, you shouldn't let the $2,000 you invested in it turn into $4,000 on the way up. You should trim the position, taking profits gradually, so that when Boeing is at 160, you own just twelve shares that are worth $1,920, about the size of your initial core position.

But guideline number one isn't enough. You still need to know when to take those profits, and that's where we use guideline number five. This one is a catchall; it tells you when you're being a pig. If you own a stock that's up 10 percent and you haven't sold any of it, you're getting piggish. If you own a stock that's up 20 percent and you haven't sold a sizable portion, you're probably a pig. If you hit a double, if a stock is up 100 percent from where you bought it, then you should sell half your position and play with the house's money, as long as you still believe in the stock. I wish I could give you a set of numbers that you could just plug in, but the truth is that while buying stocks is a science, selling stocks is more of an art.

That's why I have guideline number six, the last one for selling a stock that's made you money and you think is still going higher. You should always be eager to take profits. A lot of people have the wrong attitude. They want to see how far they can ride the stock up. That's undisciplined and it'll lose you money. If I tell you to buy a stock on *Mad Money*, then if it goes up, I want you to be eager to sell. This goes against most people's instincts, but as I said before, beating your instincts is half the battle when you're trying to invest wisely. If you buy a stock and it's up 7 percent and you can't decide whether you should take profits or not, if it's a tie between sell or no sell, then the tie-breaking vote, coming straight from me, should be to sell some of that stock.

With these six guidelines, you should be able to take profits the right way and bring your money home to the bank. I know this seems like a ridiculous topic to belabor. Why should I spend all this time talking about how to sell stocks that have gone up when you've essentially already made that money? I'll tell you why: nobody thinks about this stuff. And just like everything else, it requires a little bit of thought; it requires a solid method. When a stock goes up, you still have decisions to make about what to do with it, and I want to give you some guidelines to make those decisions easier. I don't want to leave you feeling like you are on your own, even when things are good and you own a great stock that's making you lots of money.

Cutting Your Losses

I try to get things right on *Mad Money*, but I'm not perfect. Some of the stocks I pick are gonna be losers. If I'm right just two-thirds of the time, then you can make a lot of money from listening to me. But that still leaves 33 percent of the time when I'm wrong. So you should know what to do with a bad stock and how to know when you've got something bad on your hands. There are a lot of different ways to know that a stock is a loser. You're doing your maintenance homework every week, so you're monitoring all the factors that affect a stock's price. If something changes—and these things change all the time—that will make a stock less valuable, then you have to sell. Even if the stock goes down, even if it's below what you originally paid for it, you have to sell.

If the original thesis, your original reason for buying a stock turns out not to be true, or if the story changes, then you probably want to cut your losses. Let's go back to the Boeing example to make this more concrete. We bought Boeing last chapter at $83.33 a share, and our reason for buying it was the strong aerospace cycle, which means in layman's terms that airlines are placing lots of orders for new planes because they need to replace the old ones. Our reason was that Airbus, Boeing's one really big competitor, was in shambles. Let's say Airbus gets its act together and starts taking market share from Boeing. You're going to be aware of this from doing your homework and reading newspaper articles about Boeing and its only competitor. Unfortunately, everybody else will know about it, too, and the stock will take a hit.

Because of this bad news about Airbus, Boeing might fall to $75. You just lost 10 percent on your initial investment. Should you cut your losses? If half of the original idea was that Boeing was going to be kicking Airbus's European butt and all of sudden Airbus starts beating Boeing, then yeah, you better cut your losses while you're down just 10 percent. That's rule number one of cutting your losses: if the reason you had for buying a stock stops being true, get out. Remember, you have to be able to explain why you like this stock to an ordinary person who knows nothing about stocks or business. If your reason evaporates, you can't do that.

But there are times when things are less clear-cut. There might be a piece of bad news that hits a stock and knocks it down too far. Boeing might drop too far after a piece of bad news hits it and be ripe for a bounce. Once again, if you're confused and don't know what to do, please, I have a radio show, I have *Mad Money,* feel free to call me during the "Lightning Round" and I will happily tell you what I think you should do and why. But I shouldn't be your only resource. If you've done your homework properly, you should be able to take whatever new piece of information has hurt the stock and integrate it with everything else you know. That should give you a clear picture of where a stock is going. But you have to act fast.

When a piece of bad news hits a stock, the analysts will generally revise their earnings estimates downward and then downgrade the stock. They often downgrade after a stock has already come down a lot, and that will knock it down even more. If something truly bad happens to your stock, you want to cut your losses before the downgrades start coming. Trust me, you'd rather sell a stock that's down 5 percent than sell a stock that's down 10 percent after the analysts get done beating it up. But how bad is bad? If a company lowers its guidance—that's just gibberish for its earnings forecast—that's bad. It's the kind of thing that will cause a wave of downgrades if a stock has any analyst coverage. You want to be ahead of that wave.

You can find my Ten Commandments of Trading and my Twenty-five Investment Rules to Live By in my last book, *Jim Cramer's Real Money: Sane Investing in an Insane World*. Some of these rules tell you when to cut your losses, no matter what you might think. For example, rule nineteen says that when big-time executives leave a company for no good reason—and spending time with the family isn't a good reason, because these people are career-driven nut-jobs who don't usually care about their families—something is probably wrong and you should sell. Consult the rules if you're unsure about whether a piece of news is bad enough to warrant selling a stock and cutting your losses.

Again, just as with profit taking, you should be eager to cut your losses. Your disposition should be to sell. At any given time there are hundreds of good opportunities in the market; there are lots of good stocks that can make you money. It's always better for you to cut your losses and sell damaged goods in order to buy a stock you have more conviction in. I know that it never feels good to sell a stock that's down, but investing isn't about feeling good; it's about making money. And trust me, you will have more fun and feel better if you sell your losers, even if they're only slightly damaged, and replace them with better stocks that have better reasons to go up. You'll make more money that way, and emotionally, you won't feel like damaged stocks are dragging you down. I say this only because everyone always wants to hold on to their stocks. They irrationally want to hold on to stocks that have made them money, and they irrationally want to hold on to stocks that have lost them money. If you want to invest well, if you want to be able to turn my recommendations on *Mad Money* into profits, you have to acknowledge that irrationality and combat it with discipline.

You should be eager to sell. Obviously, you want to sell into strength, which means sell when a stock is going up, but don't wait forever for a stock to rally if it's something that you don't believe in anymore. If you take my recommendations on the show, you do your homework, you buy the stocks the right way, and then you sell them the right way, that's an almost surefire recipe for profit. But if you don't believe me, if you think my show is a joke or just for entertainment, let me give you my credentials—not from my years as a money manager, but from the show. I'm going to go through my best calls and tell you what went right, as examples of good stock picking and good decision making, and also, despite the pettiness, to defend my reputation. To be fair, I'll also give you my worst calls on the show, a kind of *Mad Money* blooper reel, because I believe in holding myself accountable. But just as we learn from success, we can also learn from massive, embarrassing failures. Now that you've mastered the process of taking a stock pick from *Mad Money* all the way from my mouth through the homework and the buying and more homework and the selling and taking your money to the bank, I want to show you what my stock picks can do for you and how the whole process has worked in the year and half that I've been doing *Mad Money.*

5

THE "LIGHTNING ROUND"

How We Do It on The Show and How You Too Can Pull It Off (And Why You Should Try)

Everybody thinks that the "Lightning Round" must be rigged. For anybody who's reading this book and hasn't seen the show, first I've gotta ask what the heck are you doing with yourself at six, nine, and midnight every weekday. Second, was the cover art on this book just so good that you had to pick it up even though you've never seen the show? But if you need a little refresher, the "Lightning Round" is the ten- to fifteen-minutes that I spend testing myself every show. It's where I take calls rapid-fire, one after the other, and people can ask me about any stock the lawyers at CNBC say it's OK to mention on air. I have zero foreknowledge of the stocks before the segment starts. I think my record is something like forty stocks in one "Lightning Round." You guys call in and I tell you straight up if it's a buy or a sell.

Now there are literally thousands of stocks on the NYSE and the NASDAQ, and every night I'm hit with twenty or more of them at random. So of course people think this game is rigged. How could I have an opinion on thousands and thousands of stocks? That's just not possible, right? It's inconceivable. No ordinary man could know all these stocks—that seems to be the conventional wisdom.

Well, I do know all of these stocks. I can't say I know all of them well. But since everyone thinks that the "Lightning Round" is rigged, I'm gonna tell you, Penn and Teller style, exactly how I manage to pull it off every single night. I'll tell you what goes through my head in the ten seconds I've got between when I hear the stock and when I have to tell you what I think of it.

You'll get an inside tour of my brain. But I know it's not enough to explain what I do in the "Lightning Round." If you're really going to believe that the game isn't rigged, I must tell you not just what I do, but how I do it. I've got three dirty little secrets, and once I tell you what they are, you'll understand exactly how I can do the "Lightning Round." But not only am I going to tell you how I do the "Lightning Round," I'm going to tell you how you can do it, too. That's the only way anyone will ever believe me: if they can do what I do every night on TV themselves. First I'll give you my own secrets, and then I'll tell you what you can do to know stocks the way I know them. I'm not promising you that you'll be able to do a Jim Cramer–style Lightning Round. In some ways, I'm a freak of nature: I really shouldn't be able to remember all of these stocks, and if you can remember them as well as I do, then you've really outdone yourself. But just because you can't do a Lightning Round as I can doesn't mean you can't come close. The real benefit to playing your own Lightning Round isn't just that, if you can pull it off, you look really smart. It's not that doing a Lightning Round makes you more attractive to members of the opposite sex, although the female callers tell me that's true! You want to do your own Lightning Round because it's a fun way to do your stock and sector homework. It's an entertaining and exciting game, but it's also educational. It gives you an incentive to learn about stocks and stay engaged that goes beyond just making more money. It improves your game. And that's really what I'm all about: I want to make stocks fun, because when you're having fun, you pay more attention, and more attention usually means more money. But before I tell you how to play your own Lightning Round, I'll tell you how I go about doing *my* Lightning Round, because the way I do it and the way you do it are going to be a little different.

So what goes through my head in the seconds between when a caller screams out booyah and tells me his stock and when I tell him what to do with it? Truth be told, a lot of things. I may play a crazy man on TV, but my approach to stocks in general is methodical, and in the "Lightning Round," it gets extramethodical because I don't have a lot of time. First I hear the stock, then I start going through my checklist. I've said it before, and I'll say it again: a stock's sector determines 50 percent of its movement. So when I hear your stock in the "Lightning Round," my first thought is always What sector does it belong to? Because I do this for a living, I have an opinion about every sector out there, especially in light of where the economy is and where I think it is going. That lets me do sector analysis at, to belabor the metaphor, lightning-fast speeds. I hear the stock, I know the sector, and then I have to answer certain questions about the sector.

First and foremost: do I like or hate the sector? If you come out with an oil stock and I love oil, I know instantly that I love that sector and probably like any stock in it. I don't have to think about the sector because I've already got an opinion on it—that means it no time. If you give me an airline or an American automaker and I hate that sector, then I don't need to do any thinking to know the stock is bad too. The odds are good that if you give me a stock in a sector I don't like, I'm gonna tell you to sell it. There are some sectors that I will generally dislike through thick and thin. I spent well over a decade hating the airlines and being right every year; it's only very recently that I've come around on them, because so many of them went bankrupt, leaving the others to cash in. The sectors I'll reject out of hand, pretty much no matter what, are the ones that are too price competitive.

That means they're sectors where companies can't charge very much money because their products are virtually interchangeable with their competitors' products, and if they raise prices they'll be undercut by a cheaper competitor and will sell nothing. Supermarkets are like this, and it keeps their gross margins incredibly low. If you call me about a supermarket, unless it's a high-growth niche business like Whole Foods, I'm telling you to sell and not thinking about it further. Commodity semiconductors, the companies that make computer chips but don't design them, have the same problem—too much competition keeps prices low. There are a lot of retailers that look like this too, and the same goes for American automakers most of the time.

But what if I don't love the sector and I don't hate it? What if I'm somewhere in the middle? Then I have to ask myself, with very little time, a whole set of other questions about the sector that your stock is in. I need to know if it's a growth sector or a stagnant, share-take sector. A growth sector is a part of the economy where the whole sector is growing. Advertising on search engines, for example, is a growth sector. Google and Yahoo! can both grow their earnings, because the market for ad space on the Internet is expanding. A stagnant, share-take sector would be something like supermarkets, where there are only so many supermarkets this country needs, and they've already been built. In a stagnant sector, the only way you grow is by taking market share from your competitors, because there are no more economic places to put new stores. In general, you'd much rather be in stocks that belong to a growth sector. For the most part I'll dismiss stocks in stagnant sectors without a second thought, which is good because in the "Lightning Round," I don't have time for a second thought.

But let's say you've given me a stock that's in a good, growth sector. Then there's a whole battery of other questions I need to answer before I can tell you to buy or sell it in good faith. If your stock is in a growth sector, I need to know if the growth of the stock is as good as the growth of the sector. If the stock is growing at 15 percent, but the sector is growing at 20 percent, then I'm not going to like the stock. It's an underperformer if it's growing more slowly than the rest of its peers. If the company passes the growth test and it's growing as fast or faster than the industry it's in, then start comparing it to other companies in the same business. I want to know what P/Es other companies in the same business have. (You remember, the price-to-earnings ratio, the P/E, is the most basic way we value stocks.) If the stock is growing faster than its competitors but has a lower P/E, then it's a slam dunk. I'd give it a triple buy—we're done, next caller.

You can see that the way I approach these stocks in the "Lightning Round" is a kind of process of elimination. As soon as I know enough to say buy or sell, I move on. But if I don't get a definitive answer, I have to keep asking myself questions about the stock. If the stock isn't a slam dunk because of higher growth but a lower multiple than its peers—and most stocks aren't slam dunks—then I have to keep thinking. What if the stock has a higher P/E multiple than the industry? That presents some difficulties. I need to know if the stock is best of breed. If it's best of breed, then it deserves a higher multiple, but if it's just OK, then its P/E is too high. How do I know if a stock is best of breed during the "Lightning Round?" There are only so many sectors, and in each sector, only one or two companies can be best of breed. At any given time, I have an opinion about what's best of breed in every single sector. That means if I hear the name of a stock and I think it's best of breed, then I don't have to spend any time comparing it to its competitors, because I've already done that beforehand and reached a decision. So if it's in a growth sector and the stock has a high P/E but it's best of breed, I'll tell you to buy. If it has a higher than average P/E but is only average for the sector, I'll tell you to sell and buy the best-of-breed company. Swap out of the mediocre stock for the best of breed—you hear that from me all the time.

We're not out of my brain yet. A stock might be in a growth sector, and it might compare favorably to its competitors, but it might be the wrong time to own anything in that sector. Before I can recommend a stock, I need to know whether its sector is vulnerable too. Remember when I told you about homework and you had to find out what things would move a stock's sector before you were allowed to buy it? Well, I need to make sure those forces aren't hurting a sector before I give you a buy in the "Lightning Round." There are a lot of sectors that are very dependent on raw costs; any business that uses plastic should be sold if "resin costs"—just more Wall Street gibberish for the cost of plastics—are high. Chemical companies make use of lots of natural gas, and they should be sold when natural gas is expensive. If the sector requires lots of iron or copper, and those prices are high, then I'll tell you to sell stocks in that industry too. As I write this, we're in a high-priced commodity environment, so I'm telling people to sell companies in sectors that are dependent on low commodity costs to make money. But if commodity prices started coming down, I'd be telling people to buy those stocks.

If only that were the end of my thought process in the "Lightning Round." There's still a lot more to go, and I don't have that many seconds to do it in. If I'm going to tell you to buy, sell, or even wimp out and go with a hold, I need to know if your stock's sector is levered to the American Federal Reserve or to BRIC. BRIC, for those of you who don't keep track of the acronyms created on Wall Street to confuse you, stands for Brazil, Russia, India, and China. In my last book, *Real Money: Sane Investing in an Insane World*. I had a chart (on page 115) that described how to buy and sell stocks based on where we are in the business cycle. I'm amending that chart now. I got it less than perfect, if not wrong, because I missed some new developments in the world. My new chart is in the back of this book. (see page 206.) I've already told you about how some sectors are responsive to the Fed. The Fed raises interest rates, and financial stocks, like banks, go down. Then "smokestack" cyclical stocks go down—good examples of these are companies like Ingersoll-Rand IR and 3M (MMM). If we're in the wrong part of the cycle for the sector your stock is in, I'm going to tell you to sell it, and I'll do that quickly. But here's where I was a little off in my last chart. Some industrial stocks that I thought were dependent on the Federal Reserve are actually now much more tied to BRIC. These are the companies that sell their industrial products to Brazil, Russia, India, and China.

In general, over the next few years, companies that do business in these four countries will be more valuable than companies that don't. The reason is that every BRIC country has a very fast-growing, developing economy. High economic growth, if we're talking about a cyclical business, a business that does well in a growing economy, is by definition good for the cyclical, industrial stocks. These countries are really hitting their stride, so cyclicals that operate there are raking in the dough. I don't want to say BRIC is always better. In a decade or two, no one will even remember what BRIC means. And in the intervening time, there might be reasons why stocks with BRIC exposure become less valuable than stocks that have nothing to do with BRIC. Brazil's economy might slow down; China might relentlessly raise interest rates; Russia, well, there's no telling what could go wrong in Russia; and India might have a nuclear war with Pakistan.

A lot of the infrastructure companies, such as Fluor FLR and Foster Wheeler FWLT are now tied to these four countries. Some of the industrial stocks that sell into BRIC, like Emerson Electric EMR and United Technologies for example, aren't as dependent on the Fed here in America as they used to be. So if you throw me one of these stocks, I can pay less attention to where we are in the business cycle as long as I know how much business the company does in BRIC. That doesn't mean they're not levered to the American business cycle at all, but they're much less levered to it than they were five years ago. If the Fed raises rates in America, for example, these stocks will be hurt less than industrial stocks with no BRIC exposure. The Fed still matters to them, but it matters much less than it used to, and I keep that in mind when I tell you whether to buy, sell, or hold your "Lightning Round" stocks. I usually know where a company stands with BRIC off the top of my head, but it shouldn't be too hard for you to figure out with a few minutes and a computer. If you go to the SEC's website, or Yahoo! Finance, or TheStreet.com, you can find the quarterly report (the 10-Qs) and the annual report (the 10-K) for any company. The vast majority of industrial stocks will break down their sales by region, and often by country, in these reports. Almost every industrial has a regional sales breakdown in its earnings reports. Those reports are where you want to look to determine how dependent an industrial stock is on the Federal Reserve in America and how dependent it is on doing business in BRIC.

Then there are some sectors that have neat tricks I can use. Banking is a great example of this. If you call me about a bank, I know that banks tend to get acquired when they sell at less than two-and-a-half times their book value. Book value is just the amount of cash a bank has, its assets minus its liabilities. If your book value is $1 billion, and your capitalization is worth $2 billion, then your company trades at twice book. That is the best way to evaluate banks. A bank is really just the sum of its assets and its liabilities, or to put it in terms you can understand, its loans and its deposits. I know that banks tend to be acquired at about two-and-a-half times book value because I closely monitor the value of all the takeovers in the sector. So if you call me about a bank, I can quickly see the book value by looking at my computers, and that lets me know in a second or two if the bank is a potential takeover target. You can do it yourself—this is information that you can pluck right off Yahoo! Finance. That way, rather than calling and asking me if I think your bank is a takeover target, you can just look at its price-to-book ratio and see for yourself. Now, two-and-a-half times book value won't always be the number banks get acquired at, but as with all my other tricks, that number is easy to figure out. Just do what I do and look at the acquisitions in banking; look at the book values of banks before they get takeover bids. They'll be below a certain number—that's the number you use.

There's one more question about the sector that I need to ask myself before I can think about the individual stock. Some sectors are dependent on government spending. There are a lot of health-care companies that make most of their money from Medicare and Medicaid checks. Other companies, like Caterpillar, make more or less money depending on how much Congress decides to throw away on federal highway bills, which don't come around every year. The defense contractors are also very dependent on government generosity for their money. Sometimes this political stuff doesn't matter, but if we're in an election year, depending on who will probably win the elections, you'll want to buy or sell certain sectors. If I thought the Democrats were going to retake Congress, I would probably tell you to sell the defense contractors, because they would cut defense spending for all but homeland security. At the same time, it would be a good bet to buy anything that makes money from Medicare or Medicaid, because you would assume the Democrats would be more likely to increase spending there.

That's all the sector analysis I do in about three seconds after I hear your stock in the "Lightning Round." I've got three more seconds after that to look at the stock itself, and then I'm pretty much out of time. If the sector is OK, I'm going to look at the stock's price. I play my own little game of "The Price Is Right." If I think the market is going higher, if I think a sell-off is unlikely, if I think this is about as low as you'll get the stock, then you get a buy. But maybe we're in a rocky, volatile market and the stock is on the expensive side. Then I'm more likely to tell you to wait for a sell-off before you buy, so you can get the stock at a lower price. Or if I'm anticipating a sell-off but not sure of it, then I'll probably give you a tepid buy and tell you to buy more if the stock goes lower.

I've got about one second left now, and there are still a few factors I need to look at before I can deliver my judgment. I need to know if there's anything that could cause the stock price to diverge from what's happening with the company. This happens all the time; it's why we can make money in the market. Stocks and the companies they represent little pieces of don't always have that much in common. If you're calling about a stock and there are about to be a bunch of initial public offerings (IPOs) in the same sector, then I'll probably tell you to sell. When the market gets flooded with new companies that all do the same thing as your company, that creates a lot of supply in that sector. This is just basic economics: when you increase the supply of a certain kind of stock, you lower the price of that kind of stock. So if there are bunch of IPOs on their way in the same sector, I'm telling you to sell that stock. (That's what I did with all the newly minted ethanol stocks in 2006.) If I think that a competitor is going to announce an earnings shortfall, I will tell you to sell the stock. This is especially important with tech stocks. Whenever a similar-looking company announces a shortfall, unless they say straight out that their shortfall was due to increased competition from a specific company, all the stocks in that sector will take a hit. A lot of the time, one company's problem is another company's gain, but that doesn't matter in the short term. So if I can see an earnings shortfall for a competitor in the near future, I'll tell you to wait until after the announcement before you buy your stock.

There are just a few more things I try to keep in mind when I'm answering your calls during the "Lightning Round." At this point, I have maybe half a second before I start looking like a know-nothing goofball if I don't answer the question soon, but I still need to go through every step of my analysis. If I know that a stock is heavily shorted, for example, then I'm more likely to tell you to buy it. A lot of people like to call in about small, speculative names that have run up quite a bit. Right now I'm thinking especially of Hansen Natural (HANS), the natural beverage company that had a huge run in 2005 and 2006. These more speculative stocks get heavily shorted—remember, shorting is just when you borrow shares of a company, sell them, and then, if you do it right, buy them back and return them at a lower price. Your profit is the difference between where you sold the shares first and the lower price you bought them back at, so the shorts are effectively betting against a stock. I don't recommend heavily shorted stocks because I dislike shorts. I do it because heavily shorted stocks are ripe for a "short squeeze." There's some authentic Wall Street gibberish that can actually make you money. A short squeeze happens when a lot of people are shorting a stock and then some piece of good news pushes it higher. The shorts panic, and in order to get out, to "cover" their short positions, they have to buy the stock. That panic buying sends the stock even higher.

If I think your stock is in for an upgrade from an analyst who covers it, I'm more likely to recommend it. If I think it's ripe for a downgrade, I'm more likely to tell you to sell. How do I know if upgrades or downgrades are coming? I'm not breaking the law and getting inside information. I don't like inside information, both because it's illegal and because it makes you sloppy. If you look at Ivan Boesky, one of the titans of trading on inside information in the 1980s and the inspiration for Gordon Gekko in the movie *Wall Street,* he tended to perform poorly whenever he didn't have inside information because he'd come to rely on it as a crutch. I don't play that game. I do, however, play a game with analysts. Most Wall Street analysts aren't that creative.

They're all pretty smart, but they also think alike, and they're bad at admitting mistakes. Let's say there's a stock, call it Google in 2004, that's covered by six analysts. Five of the analysts have sell ratings on the stock, and one of them has a buy rating on it, meaning five of them think the stock is going lower and one thinks it's going higher. Then the stock doubles over the course of three or four months. Five analysts got it wrong, and one analyst got it right. In most circumstances, it's easy to game the analysts and predict what they'll do. The five guys who told you to sell Google as it was doubling are all going to upgrade the stock. It's their way of saving face and admitting they got it wrong. Keep in mind that almost all analysts have been trained exactly the same way, so they think in lockstep. The analysts aren't going to upgrade Google because they think it's going higher. They're just trying to hide their shame for getting it wrong; they're trying to

show that even though they misunderstood the stock, they understand it now. In most cases, they get it wrong again.

But this gives us a good rule of thumb that I use in the "Lightning
Round," and with stock analysts in general. If analysts are negative
about a stock and it goes up, they will upgrade it and move it even
higher. If they're positive on a stock and it goes down by a lot, they'll
downgrade it and move it even lower. There are other things that
move analysts, and if you're faster than the analysts, you can make
money from their upgrades and downgrades. Let's say Ingersoll-Rand
(IR), a solid industrial manufacturer, comes out with a better than
expected quarter and also raises its earnings forecasts for the year. If,
at the same time, there are a half-dozen analysts who have negative,
sell ratings on the stock, those analysts are going to have to flip-flop
and give the stock an upgrade. But they won't all do it at once, right
after Ingersoll-Rand reports. Some of them will try to tough it out
and maintain their sell ratings for a little longer. Eventually these guys
will have to upgrade the stock, because they got it wrong, and when
they do, the stock goes higher because analysts move stocks. You don't
always get this gap between a good quarter and an analyst upgrade,
but when I see one of these opportunities in a stock I get a call about,
I'll usually jump all over it and tell you to buy. And in general, if I have
a good feeling that an upgrade or a downgrade is coming, I always
factor this into my answer in the "Lightning Round."

OK, I'm down to maybe my last tenth of a second after hearing the
ticker symbol, and I still need to consider one thing before I can give
you a buy, sell, or, in some rare cases, a hold on the stock you asked
about: what's the management like? If I like management and the
stock has passed all the other tests, then it's a buy. If I don't like management, that's a black mark on the stock. It's hard to quantify the
value of good management, but I don't think it can ever be overesti-
mated. The real problem is that it's a subjective judgment. Luckily,
I've been in this game for a long time, and I'm familiar with most
management teams, at least for the large- and mid-cap (meaning the

large- and mid-sized) companies that I get asked about. If I don't know the management at all but I like the sector and the stock seems to have good growth and good prospects, I'll probably tell you to swap out of it. Even though the company looks good, if I know nothing about management, I don't often feel comfortable recommending the stock. Plus, there will usually be a similar stock, in the same sector, with the same or better growth, where I do know and like the management. It would be irresponsible if I didn't tell you to swap out of the company where I don't know management and swap into the similar-looking company where I like the management.

And that's it. That's all the analysis I do to come up with my buy, sell, or hold recommendations during the "Lightning Round." Now I said it takes me ten seconds to do this analysis, but if it took you only ten minutes to read through the entire process, then you read very quickly. If somebody told me they could do all of the above in ten seconds, I would be skeptical if not downright suspicious. You should be thinking that I have to be superhuman, or a liar, or a superhuman liar to pull this off. You're right to be skeptical; nobody ever got rich by being credulous. But since it's my credibility that's on the line, and since I think that you too can do your own Lightning Round if you're willing to put in the effort, I'm going to tell you how I manage to pull off this kind of detailed analysis, something that should take the better part of an hour, in just a few seconds. I have three big secrets, three tricks that let me stay ahead of the game. For the first time ever, I'm going to share them with you.

How I Pull Off the "Lightning Round": Three Secrets

Finally, you're about to see the dark underbelly of *Mad Money,* all my dirty little secrets exposed. First secret: it's been my job to know stocks for more than two decades, first as a broker, then as a money manager, then as a journalist and alleged guru. In two decades you encounter a lot of stocks. I've probably owned, at one time or another, a solid chunk of the stocks I'm asked about during the "Lightning Round," maybe even the majority of the stocks I'm asked about. You just rack up experience and it sticks with you. Plus, since I still follow the market professionally for CNBC, *RealMoney Radio*, and TheStreet.com, where I run the ActionAlertsPLUS.com portfolio, which is also my charitable trust, I need to stay ahead of the game. It's my job to know which sectors I like and which sectors I hate. It's my job to know which management teams are good and bad, to know when a short squeeze or an upgrade is on the way, to know which stocks are best of breed, and to help you use that information to get rich. That means I've done a lot of this analysis ahead of time, even though I don't know any of the stocks in the "Lightning Round" in advance.

OK, I know, that can't explain everything. That first secret was intentionally unsatisfying. I've got a second dirty little secret—this one is more of a guilty pleasure, actually. Stocks aren't just my job, they're also my favorite hobby. Some people golf for fun, some people drink, I listen to quarterly conference calls the way other people watch baseball games. Even if I had no money on the line, even if I didn't have my television show, I would still follow all of these stocks because it's just fun for me. Maybe my memory with these stocks is freakish, but don't you know anybody who has some freakish ability to remember baseball statistics? Have you ever had a friend who could tell you the ERA of every single pitcher in Major League Baseball? My memory with stocks is a little like that. I think the comparison to sports is actually perfect. There are thousands of stocks, and there are around a thousand professional baseball players. There are fourteen teams in the American League, sixteen teams in the National League, and every team has a twenty-five or forty-man roster, depending on the time of year. That comes out to as many as twelve hundred players. I'm sure there aren't a lot of baseball fans who know everybody in both leagues, in fact there may not be any, but I'm also sure that diehard fans know a lot about a lot of players. I'm a big stock fan, and with a couple thousand stocks out there that I can legally talk about on the show (I'll tell you about CNBC's legal restrictions later in the chapter), it's not that hard or unpleasant for me to follow them closely. I know that's still a totally unsatisfying explanation, even if it helps to explain some of why I've done this analysis in my head beforehand. Again though, if you're a baseball fan, don't you have an opinion about Joe Torre, the manager of the Yankees? Don't you know what you think of Barry Bonds? So the stock market fan factor is actually a big part of why I can pull off the "Lightning Round."

But there's another factor, a third dirty little secret behind the "Lightning Round." It's really not that I'm cheating. I know you wanted me to say that, but it's just not true. The third secret is that it's easier than it looks. You don't have to know every little detail about every little stock to have an opinion about it. You don't need to know a stock inside out to be right about whether it's going up or down. All you need to know is what sector that stock belongs to and where it stands within the sector. It could be a health-care stock, it could be a steel stock, it could be an oil stock, it could be a transportation stock, it could be a tech stock, or maybe a bank or an automaker. If you know which sector a stock belongs to, and you've got an opinion about that sector, then you've got an opinion about that stock. There've been academic studies, studies that are actually worth all the wasted time and money that goes into the academy, that prove that half of a stock's movement comes from its sector. Half of what a stock does, and I confirm this from my own empirical experience with the market, is related just to what business the stock is in. Makes sense, right?

So on the "Lightning Round," let's say you call me about some obscure bank. I don't know a lot of details about the bank, it's a stock I've barely ever heard anything about. But I know it's a bank, and that means it makes its money the way every other bank does, by lending people money and making a profit off of the interest. I don't know the CEO or the CFO of this hypothetical bank, I don't know its growth rate, I don't know its multiple, but I know it's a bank. Can I give you good advice about it on the "Lightning Round"? You bet. Remember that 50 percent number: 50 percent of what a stock does comes straight out of its sector. So I know that whichever way the banks are going, the odds are very, very good that this obscure bank is going to move in that direction too.

Now, it's the "Lightning Round," I get a call about this obscure bank, and I'm about to dispense some sage advice about the stock. I need one more thing: I need a solid opinion about what the banks are going to do. So suppose that the Federal Reserve is raising interest rates, which means the rate banks borrow at is going up, which means the rate they lend to you has to increase for the banks to keep making profits, which also means they're going to make fewer loans because people hate borrowing money at higher interest rates. Hey, that means bank stocks should be doing pretty badly, right? So now I've got an opinion about banks, I think that they're headed down because we've got rate hikes as far as the eye can see. So you call me about your bank, and even though it's not a bank I have much experience with, I'm confidently going to tell you to sell it.

Not only will I tell you to sell it with confidence, but I'll probably be right. If all the banks are going down, if the sector is going down, then on average, and always keep this in mind, half of what your bank stock does will be to go down, and go down hard. Even if it's the best bank in the world, that determines only about half of its fate. If banking is going down hard, then this stock had better be the best bank ever created with the most brilliant management and the most innovative business model, otherwise it's going down too. And if this was the best bank on earth, then let me tell you something—it wouldn't be some obscure bank I'd never heard of; it would be something that was on a lot of people's radars; it'd be a stock I knew a lot about. As it stands, obscure stocks tend not to be best of breed.

If there are any tricks behind the "Lightning Round," that's by far and away the biggest one: I can tell you what a stock will do if I'm right about the sector, and I'm usually right about the sector. I've done all the sector analysis beforehand, because even though there are thousands of stocks, there aren't that many sectors. And having that sector analysis done before I start thinking, before the clock in my head starts ticking down, means I can use my time in the "Lightning Round" to go through the specifics of a stock, if it passes the sector test. That's the big secret.

To be totally fair, I do get a lot of stocks wrong in the "Lightning Round." It's not as rigorous as some of the other segments on *Mad Money*, where I really crack down, do my homework, and give you a lot of hard facts about why you should like or hate a company. Remember, we don't love stocks—they're just pieces of paper. But it's OK to hate pieces of paper—I've always been a believer in the power of hate. Even though the "Lightning Round" is a bit of a game, even though it's not as rigorous as the rest of *Mad Money*, I'm still right more often than I'm wrong. I still think you should listen to what I'm saying; I'm just not necessarily saying it as emphatically as I would if I had all day to research the stock and then five or ten minutes to lay out the case for it, as I do with some of my other segments.

That sector trick is something you can do at home; it's one way you can learn how to play the Lightning Round as I do. But before I tell you how to play the Lightning Round at home, I want to give you an idea of what it's like behind the scenes of the "Lightning Round" on *Mad Money*. Too many people have said too many times that it's rigged; I owe it to them to provide a satisfactory explanation of what's going on. So let me give you the whirlwind tour of the "Lightning Round" and the *Mad Money* phone room.

Behind the Scenes of the "Lightning Round"

I have to confess, I really had no idea how the "Lightning Round" works behind the scenes until I asked my staff about it for this book. The mechanics of the "Lightning Round" are kept secret from me, just as everything about the callers and their questions is kept secret from me. I want the "Lightning Round" to be totally authentic, and in order to keep it authentic, I've kept myself in the dark even about the harmless mechanical details of the process. I really don't want anyone to question the validity of the process, and I don't want anyone to accuse me of cherry-picking. That's why I avoid the whole shooting match in the phone room, because I don't want to create even the slightest impression that the integrity of the process has been compromised. When it comes to the mechanics of the "Lightning Round" on my end, all I have is a screen with a list of names and states and the name of the stock the instant I call the name of the viewer. I just call them out in the order the phone room gives me. That way the "Lightning Round" is just me without any help, except from my computers, which I barely have any time to use anyway. That's why I make mistakes every now and then, or don't know a stock, to my perpetual chagrin.

But if you want to know how it works, here's what my producers tell me. During the day people call in, they leave messages in the *Mad Money* voice-mail box—I'm sure many of you have been through this process. Then my staff calls them back and tells them to call right before we film the show. Once you guys call back, you listen to a really long disclaimer about personal investment advice, and CNBC's liability, and all that other boring stuff, and then you talk to my amazing phone-room staff. These guys take down the names of callers, they take down where they're from, and then they take down the stock names. They also vet the stocks.

Vetting the stocks isn't some shady, corrupt thing. I have absolutely nothing to do with vetting the stocks. The legal department at

CNBC doesn't want me ever to talk about stocks with a market cap—that's the value of each share times the number of shares outstanding, or the total market value of the company—below $250 million. If the stock is under $5 a share then the market cap must be more than $500 million. At CNBC, the standing policy is that we're not allowed to talk about stocks this small unless there's some really compelling reason, because any mention of a stock that small on TV, even on shows without a following like *Mad Money*'s, would move the stocks too much. I didn't make these requirements, the legal department did. I'll admit, they make it a lot easier for me. If I was just getting call after call about tiny little stocks, I'd probably miss a ton of them, because I'm much more familiar with larger companies and pay very little attention to micro-cap stocks—that's authentic Wall Street gibberish for these small companies. So the rules do make it easier for me, but they're not my rules.

Now you're wondering: the phone room is vetting these stocks and making a list of them. Where does that list go? Does this list go to me? Absolutely not. The list goes to another producer on the show, who then prepares the graphics and the charts. I say my staff prepares the graphics on the fly, and I mean it. They're typing in names and stocks during the "Lightning Round" to get them on the screen. I don't know the stocks until I hear the caller say his or her name. That's why every now and then I mishear, and I talk about the wrong stock. Once that happened with a stock called Coherent (COHR)—the stock was coherent, but the caller wasn't.

So there it is, that's how I approach the "Lightning Round," the tricks I use to pull off that approach, and the behind-the-scenes magic that brings it all together. Next I'll tell you the rules for the Lightning Round Home Game and give you some tips so you can impress your friends, relatives, and acquaintances with your knowledge about stocks. But there's more to the home game than just plain fun. There's a payoff beyond just looking smart. The more you practice your own Lightning Round, the better you will get at sector analysis; that's really the heart of the game. You have to develop opinions about every sector, and you have to follow those sectors if you're going to be any good at doing your own Lightning Round. The game also forces you to rank the top stocks in each sector. You know how the Atkins diet was really just a way to trick people into eating fewer calories by telling them to binge on high-protein, high-fat foods? Well, my Lightning Round Home Game is a way of tricking you into doing your homework. If you want to have fun and really impress your friends, you've gotta have all that stuff in your head. You'll become an expert on every sector out there. Normally, that would feel like a long, boring, and horribly tedious process. But when you play the Lightning Round yourself, learning all those sectors in preparation becomes fun and challenging. You know what I say: when you're having fun, it's a lot easier to make money.

6

THE LIGHTNING ROUND
HOME GAME

Stock Market
Strength Training

Let's be honest: you want to be me. Maybe you'd want to be a little taller, or a little better looking, although I don't know why, but when it comes to stocks, if you're reading this book, I'm assuming that you aspire to be as good as I am. And hey, I don't blame you. I made a lot of money in the market. I made that money by being able to decide what I wanted to focus on and what I wanted to ignore. There are six or seven thousand stocks out there, and if you can't narrow your focus, you can't win. Coincidentally, the "Lightning Round" is a distillation of what I would do in my investment meetings with analysts at my old hedge fund. It's a way to order and make sense of the market. That's why trying to play along with me on the show, or playing your own private Lightning Round, is a great way to turn yourself into a professional-level investor. That's why I think learning how to play your own Lightning Round isn't just about having fun, it's one of the best ways to become truly great at making money in the market.

There are two ways to play the Lightning Round at home. There's the regular Lightning Round Home Game, and then there's the advanced version. These two Lightning Rounds are virtually identical, but the rules are a little different. So first I'll explain the rules of each Lightning Round, and then I'll tell you how I think you should approach them if you want to make friends and impress people.

In the regular version, you get fifteen seconds to come up with a buy, sell, or hold for each stock. You can play along with the show or with a crowd, or just a couple of friends—that doesn't matter. After you come out with your judgment, you can spend as much time as you want talking about why you like or dislike the stock, but you can't stop. As soon as you stop, you have to go to the next stock. When I do the "Lightning Round," as I mentioned before, the legal department at CNBC prevents me from taking questions on stocks smaller than $250 million in market capitalization. If you want to do your own Lightning Round, you should probably follow my legal department's example and avoid these small-cap names too, because anybody can stump you with some little $20 million company no one's ever heard of. That said, it's perfectly OK to speculate on companies that are worth less than $250 million, but remember, you're only allowed to put 20 percent of your portfolio in speculative stocks, and only if you're a big risk taker.

But let's get back to the Lightning Round. In the regular version you get a computer. You get the Internet. In that fifteen seconds, you're allowed to hit up Yahoo! Finance, or MSN Money, or TheStreet.com and look up anything you want. You can look up the stock. I have a whole desk full of computers in front of me when I do the "Lightning Round." You get to use the same resources. Believe me, with fifteen seconds, if you know nothing about the stock or the sector it's in, you won't be able to figure out if the stock is a buy or a sell just by looking at its page on Yahoo! Finance. You won't even be able to get a good handle on what the company does. You can use the computer, but you can't rely on it. Maybe there's a piece of information you weren't aware of that will help sway your decision, like the price-to-book value of a bank, or the stock's dividend yield, but that's about all you'll have time to pull off of the Web in fifteen seconds. I have even less time than you do, and I have that crazy music blaring in my ears, so even though you can use the computer in the easier version of the home game, it's there only to help broaden your analysis, to give it a little extra detail. The computer can't make your decision for you, and it can't give you enough information to compensate for the fact that you don't know a stock. It's not a crutch, just a very weak cane.

In the advanced version of the Lightning Round Home Game, you get no computer. You're out there without a rope, without a lifeline, without any external source of information that can give you good data points. It's harder, but it's still something you can pull off if you follow my advice. That's the only difference between the regular and the advanced home games. Now I'll tell you how you can excel at both.

First, for everyone who doesn't feel up to the task: being able to do your own Lightning Round is a great way to become familiar with stocks; it's one of the best ways to learn how to do good sector-based analysis, but it's by no means essential to becoming a good investor. This method isn't for everyone. It's very time-consuming—it takes way more than that one hour per week per stock of homework you're supposed to be doing. But if you really want to take control of your finances, if you really want to free yourself from brokers and investment advisers, then please don't just treat this chapter as a game. Take its lessons to heart. You can still make a lot of money if you don't train to do your own Lightning Rounds. It will put you at the top of your game, but you don't have to be at the top of your game to make money. If you watch the show, if you take my advice—although always with a grain or two of salt—and you do your preliminary homework on every stock and an hour of maintenance homework on that stock every week, then I'm confident you'll beat most managers out there.

But if you want to go above and beyond what's necessary, if you want to be great, then training for the Lightning Round Home Game might be the best way for you to make yourself a real stock-market expert. There's an easy way for you to train yourself to do the kind of analysis I do whenever I get a phone call. It's methodical and straight-forward. There are three easy steps to preparing yourself for a Light-ning Round. First you must know what all the sectors are. This isn't as easy as it looks because there are a lot of different ways to slice up the economy. You'll want to make a list of every sector and the subsectors that each one is composed of. If this seems daunting, I'll show you how it's done. Let me give you a brief example of the difference be-tween a sector and a subsector or industry. One sector, broadly speak-ing, is technology. Within the tech sector, you can find a bunch of different subsectors: the Internet, semiconductors, PCs, device mak-ers (think cell phones), and software, to name a few. You can break these subsectors down further—software, for example, really begs to be divided further—but at some point you have to draw the line or you'll end up having to form an opinion about every single stock. The whole point of the Lightning Round is that you need to have only a small number of opinions about sectors and subsectors. So for the most part, I would err on the side of not cutting things up into too many different industries, because that just creates more work for you. At a certain point, that work stops paying off. But don't get too caught up in this now; I'll walk you through all three steps in detail after I outline the process.

Step two: you'll want to form opinions about each sector and its subsectors so that when someone asks you about a stock, and you know which sector it falls into, you will instantly know how you feel about the sector, and thus how you feel about the stock. That's the biggest time-saver. I'll tell you how to form opinions about each sec-tor. It's really not all that different from step two of your homework, where you have to figure out which sector a stock belongs to and then look at all the factors that affect the value of stocks in that sector. If you want to do your own Lightning Round, must update your opinions frequently because the market is dynamic, and a sector that's in favor one day might be out of favor the next.

Once you have an opinion about each sector, you're ready for step three: rank the stocks in each subsector. You don't have to rank every stock there is—that would be waste of your time. The amount of time you spend ranking stocks within subsectors will depend on how much effort you want to put into this game and into making yourself into a general stock-market expert. At minimum, you should form an opinion about which stocks are best of breed in each subsector. If you know what's best of breed, then anytime someone asks you about a stock in that industry or subsector, you can just tell them, with confidence, to swap out of their stock and into best of breed. Now, I don't want you to get bogged down by this idea of best of breed. Remember, flexibility is always king. What's best of breed one day might be worst of breed the next. You always have to be ranking and reranking these sectors. In tech, for example, best of breed doesn't really exist, because the market for tech is too fluid. But at any given moment, you can have an opinion about what's working best and what isn't working. At the very least, you should know what you like best in each industry, so that if someone asks you about something in that industry, you can use your favorite stock as a reference point. But if you want to invest more time into the home game, you can be even more thorough. You could form a list of the top two or top three stocks in each subsector. But the best use of your time might be to break down each subsector into different categories of stocks. Know what's best of breed in the industry, then also find a stock in the sector that you think represents the best takeover target, then find another one that might be the best speculative stock in the subsector. That way, if someone asks you about a pharmacy, for example, you could have a stable of different suggestions. If you get asked about a big, stable pharmacy like CVS (CVS), you could tell the person to swap out of CVS and into the best of breed pharmacy, Walgreens (WAG). But if you get asked about Longs Drug Stores (LDG), which is a much smaller, much less established drug-store chain, then you could say that Walgreens is best of breed, but if your friend wants to own a more speculative drug store, the one to buy isn't Longs, it's Rite Aid (RAD). You need to know only that WAG is the best pharmacy and RAD is the best small-cap, speculative stock in the pharmacy business in order to give those two very good Lightning Round answers.

If you follow these three steps, then you'll be able to pull off a great Lightning Round, either with a computer or without one. I won't lie to you and say that this is an easy thing that takes no time. It'll take you more than an hour of homework a week to be able to have an opinion about every sector and to know what's best of breed in all those sectors, but the payoff is tremendous. You won't just be able to do your own Lightning Round. You will be totally on top of every single sector. You'll have a comprehensive understanding of the entire market. I can't stress enough how valuable that is. But if you don't enjoy the stock game that much, or you don't have a lot of time, then playing the Lightning Round Home Game is a distraction you don't need. You ought to focus on what counts most if you want to make money. I don't want you to spend a lot of time trying to become good at the Lightning Round before you do your weekly homework. The regular homework comes first. Owning five to ten stocks in a diversified portfolio and doing the research on them is what you absolutely must focus on to make money. But if you have the extra time and the inclination, playing the Lightning Round will make you a better investor. And a Lightning Round board game with an egg timer may be my next project.

So let's get to business. To make step one easy for you, I'll tell you how I would break up the market into sectors and then I'll identify industries within each sector. Here's a quick and easy breakup of the economy into sectors, and sectors into subsectors. This should make you job a lot easier. I'm not going to pretend that this is a thorough and canonical way to slice and dice the market, but as long as you're flexible and careful about grouping companies into their respective industries, I'm sure you'll be able to take care of step one easily.

Sectors
Aerospace
Automobiles
Consumer goods
Defense contractors
Financial
Food and beverage
Health care
Housing
Industrials
Metals and minerals
Oil and gas
Paper and chemicals
Retail
Services
Technology
Transports
Utilities

These are the big-picture sectors that people usually talk about. Some of them are self-contained and make a lot of sense internally, but some make no sense whatsoever. Tech, for example, isn't really a sector. Tech stocks do trade together—there's no question about that—but "tech" is really a twentieth-century designation. There used to be a lot less software, a lot fewer gadgets, and no good way to make money from the Internet. Now all of that's changed. I defy anyone to tell me what Google (GOOG), which makes the vast majority of its money from selling advertising on its searches, and KLA-Tencor (KLAC), a company that makes the machines that make semiconductors, have in common. On the other hand, autos,

aerospace, and defense contractors are much more sensible group-
ings. There are only a handful of big defense contractors. There
are only a handful of big automakers. These companies can be compared easily, and that makes your life easier if you're trying to play
your own Lightning Round.

But don't be fooled by this list of sectors. If you know just one
great stock for each of the seventeen sectors on that list, you're not
ready. Take the financial sector. This includes banks, investment
banks, and discount online brokerages—not to mention savings and
loans and credit-card companies. Being able to do a Lightning Round
means having a feel for each of these subsectors. You should be able
to look at the sectors, which represent only so much, and cut them up
into smaller industries that are more meaningful. Transports is another good example. Transports could include trucking companies,
railroads, airlines, and any company that services those businesses.
These things don't all trade together. Same with health care. Big
pharma, biotech, and HMOs don't all trade together either. So when
I talk about sector analysis, what I'm really talking about is industry
analysis. If you just look at the sector, you won't do enough work, and
you won't be able to do a good Lightning Round. Knowing the subsector a company actually is in, and not just the sector that it's a part
of, can also help you stay diversified. If you know exactly what a business does, and not just that it's part of the financial sector or the tech
sector, then you'll be much better able to avoid having too many similar-looking stocks. You won't get caught in a situation where you're
not diversified because you'll have a thorough understanding of what
companies actually do and what they're really levered to.

Obviously just as I don't expect you to be familiar with every sin-
gle publicly traded company to play the Lightning Round Home
Game, you don't have to be familiar with every industry out there.
But before you play, you should have a handle on most of them. If you
can know fifty or sixty industries, then I think you're in good shape.
But which industries should you know? Standard & Poor's uses

147 different subgroups to break up sectors into individual industries. That's a lot. You could start by going through this list and writing off industries that seem small, unimportant, or uninteresting, but I think that's the wrong approach. You don't need to look at a list to know that airline services doesn't seem like a big industry, nor does retail real estate investment trusts. I think your best strategy is to be reactive. Don't try to create a spreadsheet with 147 different industries and your pick for best-of-breed stock in each. That's a waste of effort, and the point of practicing to do your own Lightning Round is to concentrate effort.

I suggest you start with what you know. The odds are good that you're already familiar with at least a handful of industries or subsectors. Unless you're a professional, you're never going to have a handle on even a majority of subsectors, but that's fine because most of the subsectors are too small to matter. This is a situation where you can actually go with your gut for once. You can rely on your intuition, but the best thing you can do is watch the show. You should watch the "Lightning Round." The stocks people call about most frequently will belong to the industries that matter most. Watch and keep track of which industries seem important and large and which ones are rarely asked about. When you notice that an industry is talked about a lot, that's one you ought to rank. Keep watching the show. Once you have at least forty different industries in your head, you know what you think of them, and you know which stocks are best within these industries, then you're ready to do a Lightning Round. Remember, playing your own Lightning Round isn't a high-stakes game. It's not about making money or losing money—it's all about practice. You'll learn by trying to do the Lightning Round. If someone comes at you with a company in an industry that you had no idea existed, that's a good thing. You'll get the question wrong, but you'll also be able to go out and figure out how the industry works and which stocks in it you like.

Once you have a handle on which industries are out there, you have to figure out what you like and what you don't like. This is actually surprisingly easy—except with tech. Tech is never easy; it can't be gamed because there's always some new product coming along to wreck all your preconceptions about the sector. But for every other sector, step two is pretty simple. You must form an opinion about each sector. Virtually every sector is levered to some kind of cycle. Most are levered to the business cycle, by which I mean the business cycle in America, since most of the stocks I deal with are American. There's a chart in the back of this book that is an amended version of a chart (see page 206) in my last book. This chart tells you which sectors to buy during which part of the cycle. Use this as a reference, but don't let it make all your decisions for you. The key to good investing, and the key to playing a good Lightning Round, is flexibility. If you're going to be a flexible investor, you have to practice being flexible. So use the chart to help you make your decisions, but be sure you know why you are following the chart. For example, the chart tells you to sell banks before the Fed starts raising interest rates. If you're playing your own Lightning Round, you could just tell people to sell all their banks because rates are increasing; that's what the chart says. But that wouldn't do you any good. The point of playing your own Lightning Round isn't just to impress your friends—you're also trying to become a better investor. You need to know that you sell banks when interest rates increase because high rates cause banks to make fewer loan and less money.

Not everything is levered to the business cycle. There is an aerospace cycle, and it's virtually independent from the business cycle. With aerospace, you can expect seven good years and seven bad years. When this book comes out, there should be about two more good years left in the latest aerospace cycle. Why does it work this way? Because the aerospace cycle is really a cycle of airplane replacement, and seven years is just how that happens to work out. Defense contractors are levered entirely to government spending. That's not really cyclical, but it is easily observed. If the Pentagon is cutting defense spending, you'll probably go negative on the defense contractors. If we're going to war, you probably want to tell people to buy them. And the farm equipment cycle is levered to grain prices, not interest rates.

In the past, metals and minerals were more tied to the U.S. business cycle, but now, as I've said previously, many of them are more levered to global business cycles because Brazil, Russia, India, and China are developing so quickly and need access to things like copper, zinc, iron, nickel, and so on. But you can pay attention to business cycles in each of the BRIC countries too—it's not that hard if you read a newspaper. By watching these cycles, you should be able to get a good handle on these stocks.

I could go through every single industry and tell you what it's levered to and how best to play it, but that's another book. It would also be impossible to write that book because everything in it would quickly become outdated. That's why I continue to prize flexibility above all else. If you're preparing for your own Lightning Round Home Game, you need to be willing to change your mind about each of these sectors. Revise your opinion—if not every week, at least every other week—or you won't be able to do a decent Lightning Round. The point here is to keep you watching sectors, to keep you watching the whole market, and to give you a fun way to hold a lot of information in your head. The real prize here is that if you can have a solid opinion about every sector and most of the subsectors or industries, then you'll really have a good feel for the market. Once you have a good feel for the market, you'll be able to make a lot more money. It's just a matter of experience. Experience is what lets me be so good at what I do, and experience will make you good at it too.

Once you've broken down the market into different sectors and industries, and only after you've come up with an opinion about each industry, then you shop for best-of-breed stocks in the industries you like. If the economy is really strong and you think that utilities are boring places to invest because their stocks have tended to do less well in a fast-growing economy, then, at least for the purposes of your own Lightning Round, you don't have to have a favorite utility. You can just tell people to sell utilities. The whole point of this sector analysis in the Lightning Round is that it makes your life easier by giving you fewer things to focus on. If, on the other hand, the economy is slowing and the Fed is raising rates, you'd want to have a favorite utility. (I like to have a favorite growth utility—Texas Utilities—and a favorite slow grower—Excelon.) But in that situation you wouldn't bother with banks or retail or most of the industrials.

That's why step three—picking best of breed in each sector—comes after step two, where you decided which sectors you like and dislike. Now if you really want to be a pro, if you, for some psychotic reason, aspire to be me, then you won't be lazy. You'll pick out best-of-breed stocks even in sectors you hate. And you'll do it in the name of flexibility. Suppose one week the autos are terrible, but the next week they turn out to be great. If you were a money manager, you'd want to know which automaker to buy as soon as you went positive on autos. But you're probably not a money manager, and right now we're not even talking about investing real money. We're playing a game, and I want to make the game easy for you, because the easier it is, the more likely you are to practice. And the more you practice, the better you get.

So how do you go about picking best of breed? Or, if we don't want to use that term, how do you pick your favorite stock in each industry? Go back to the beginning of this book and read through all the stock analysis I talked about there. Look at how stocks are priced relative to their competitors. Compare them based on their P/E multiples and their growth rates. Take into account their future prospects; which is most consistent and least prone to earnings misses? Once you've done that, you can declare one stock your favorite. Now be warned, this could take a lot of time. You might have to study a lot of stocks before you decide on a favorite, and that's just in one industry. The payoff, however, is that you'll get really good at comparing stocks, and you'll also develop an in-depth understanding of the sector you're looking at. Plus, if you want to impress your friends, you'll be able to do your own Lightning Round right in front of them.

The method I outlined at the beginning of this book is what you want to use here in step three of practicing for your own Lightning Round. I'm fixed on this point because there will always be some temptation to base your stock judgments entirely on your interactions with companies in your everyday life. The legendary Peter Lynch popularized this style of investing: "invest in what you know." By that logic, your favorite bank should be your local bank if it looks like it's well run and popular. Your favorite retailer should be the local retailer that looks most crowded. Same goes for your favorite restaurant stock. Peter Lynch is one of the greatest investors of all time, and I'm turning his philosophy into a straw man so I can demolish it, but I'm doing that for a reason. A lot of people will make the mistakes I've just outlined. I myself will often recommend that people invest in their own local banks because they know them. There's an enormous caveat there, though, that often is left out: don't invest in your local bank if it's a bad stock. We're just talking practice right now; we're not talking real investments. This is just a game. But if you want to invest like a pro and you want to use your own Lightning Round to train your way up there, then you can't do the Lightning Round wrong.

At the end of the day, it's the numbers that matter. Your own perceptions of a company can and will deceive your more often than not. I urge you not to be deceived. Rely on the numbers. Or, as I say on the show, the anecdotal doesn't matter much on *Mad Money*. Use the earnings and the growth rates of companies to compare them, not how they appear to stack up next to one another in your day-to-day interactions with them. Once you've come up with a favorite stock in each industry, you need to reevaluate that opinion at least weekly, just as you reevaluate your opinion of each sector. The stock market is dynamic. Your favorite stock might implode, or it might go up so much that it becomes too expensive and you prefer to recommend a different company in the same sector. As long as you keep monitoring the situation and you keep practicing, you should be able to pull off a Lightning Round as well as I do. I know that all of this seems incredibly labor-intensive and time-consuming. As I said before, doing the homework to be able to pull off a Lightning Round is not for everyone. But doing all this extra work can save you a lot of time in the future, because you'll have an amazingly thorough understanding of what kind of stocks you want, when you want them, and why you own them. Doing the homework for a Lightning Round, long term, means you need to do less homework to prepare to buy individual stocks because you'll already understand what affects their sector and industry, and you'll already know how those stocks rank within their peer group.

Just remember that the Lightning Round is all about sector analysis. After that it's an easy game of stock picking within sectors. If you want to do your own Lightning Round to broaden your knowledge of the market, just make sure you understand what all the sectors and industries are, know which industries you like and which ones you don't, know your favorite stock in each of your favored industries, and always, always, always update your opinions.

Even when you become really good at doing your own Lightning Round, you're still going to get stumped every now and again. Even I get stumped. If you're confident that you've mastered the method I just discussed and somebody throws you a stock you don't know, that's a really bad sign. If you don't know the stock, you can't really say it's a sell. That said, for me it is often a triple-sell. I was once asked about a paving company called Astec (ASTE) that I'd never heard of. I answered "I don't know," and took a pass. Two days later the stock blew up. Remember, preparing for the Lightning Round is about trying to figure out which stocks are easy, which stocks are too hard, and which stocks are just plain not fun. If you don't recognize a stock, definitely think twice about buying it, because once you're an expert at the Lightning Round, it's probably too hard and not fun.

I know that when you watch me do a Lightning Round, it looks like I'm just making snap judgments about stocks. But as you can see, that couldn't be farther from the truth. You never want to make a snap judgment because you'll usually be wrong as the stock market's just too hard for that. The Lightning Round is really about creating your own stock worldview. It's about figuring out which sectors are working right now and which sectors could be working six to twelve months from now, depending on a number of factors, but primarily the actions of the Federal Reserve and inflation expectations. Once you have that worldview—and as you can see, creating it takes a lot of time and effort—you can graft your own level of comfort with risk on top of it. Then when you hear a stock, either on my show or when you're playing your own Lightning Round, you can use your stock worldview to quickly, almost instantly, develop an opinion about a stock.

Let me give you one last word of encouragement. You've got a lot more time to do your Lightning Round than I have when I'm on air. That means you can get more work done. You can spend more time thinking about a stock or looking up some of its details on the computer. You're in what I like to think of as a booyah-free zone, like my Sudden Death segment at the end of the show. You don't have to spend any time socializing with the people you're playing with; you can just focus on the stocks. That gives you a big edge, and a big head start on me, and that's good for morale. So if you think you're up for it, if you want to become a truly great investor, and (most important) if you've got the time, go train up to be a Lightning Round champion. I guarantee it'll help you make money.

7

WHY AND HOW
YOU SHOULD WATCH MY
CEO INTERVIEWS

Almost every night I bring a CEO or a CFO on to my show to interview about his stock. This is a standard feature of most financial shows, but *Mad Money* isn't a standard show by any stretch of the imagination. It seems pretty obvious why I'd bring a CEO on the show: if you're going to own a stock, wouldn't you want to hear from management? I can actually think of a lot of reasons why not. You absolutely cannot watch my CEO interviews without understanding their real purpose. I'm not trying to get these people on for information. It's actually much more subtle than that. CEOs aren't legally allowed to break news on television. There's a rule set down by the SEC, Regulation FD (Fair Disclosure), that makes it illegal for publicly traded companies to disclose new information through any medium other than a press release. So you can't watch these guys in the hopes that they'll give you some new piece of information. That's off the table, although the rest of the media doesn't understand that and continually makes you feel that news is broken in these interviews, which causes you to trade on old information that the big boys already know about. That's disinformation, but it happens because the general media doesn't understand the sea change that FD caused.

I don't bring on CEOs to try to make news; I bring on CEOs to try to make you money. But you can't make money from these interviews if you don't know what to look for. And you can't know what to look for if you don't understand what I'm trying to do when I bring these guys on.

Before I tell you how these interviews can make you money, let me first give you a word of caution. Most of the CEOs I've brought on the show are decent, honest people. They're not out to bamboozle anyone. But that said, a CEO usually gets paid by the performance of his or her stock, so you're not going to hear much in the way of negativity from most executives. So when you watch these interviews, and you hear an executive sounding very enthusiastic about his company, you should temper your optimism. These guys aren't lying, but it's their job to promote the stock. There's nothing wrong with any of this, so long as you keep these facts in mind when you watch my interviews. Just compare it to politics. A CEO is like a presidential candidate. Would you ever have expected John Kerry or George Bush to come out and say "Don't vote for me?" Or beyond that, "Don't vote for me, let me lay out twenty reasons why I'd make a terrible president?" Of course not; it's their job to sell themselves. For the same reason, you'll almost never catch a CEO saying "Don't buy my stock." It's their job to keep that stock price high and keep shareholders happy.

So given the fact that CEOs can't break news, and given the fact that they're liable to put a little positive spin on things, how do you make money from my interviews? There are four different ways these interviews can make you money and five ways they can help you not lose money. If you know how to watch, I guarantee these interviews will be very helpful.

Often I'll bring on a CEO just because I like the stock and the story behind it and I just want you to buy the darn thing. I bring the CEO on as an endorsement of the stock. These are the stocks that would've been sure buys for my hedge fund, stocks that might ultimately get added to my charitable trust, ActionAlertsPlus.com. How do you know when you're getting one of these interviews? You know that because at the end of the interview, I hit that bull button, followed by the BUY BUY BUY button. That's your Cramer seal of approval. It means you can and should buy the stock now. It tells you that I've done the homework for you and it's safe to buy. Of course you should always be doing your homework—that's a rule. But there are times when I'm so familiar with a company and so confident it'll do well, that once I've brought on the CEO for reassurance, I'm almost willing to waive your homework requirement. I will never give that kind of green light unless I've brought the CEO on TV and had a chance to talk with him on camera. The reason for that is pretty simple—if a CEO bags me, if he comes on and says things are great when they're really terrible, he's got himself a little problem. Most CEOs are honest and straightforward with me for no other reason than that they're good guys. But some are honest out of fear. I have *Mad Money*, I have TheStreet.com, I have my column in *New York* magazine, and I have my *Real Money* radio show. If a CEO messes with me on the show, if he tries to mislead me, he knows that I can and will come after him for it. They all know that I have lots of venues to exact revenge and that I will use them. I'll bury him nationally, on- and off-line. That's why you can trust that most of the CEOs on the show are credible. But again, most of them would be credible no matter what.

Let's get back to the main idea here: what does it look like when I bring on a CEO as a golden endorsement of his stock? What does a Cramer-seal-of-approval interview look like? Let me give you an example of a really great interview that made people a lot of money so you'll be able to recognize this kind of thing in the future. A classic example of a high-enthusiasm interview was when I brought on Bill

Greehey, then the CEO of Valero (VLO), the largest refiner in the United States. If you want to look for a seal of approval, look no further than this interview. The day before I brought Greehey on the show, I had a chance to talk to him one-on-one as part of the booking process. He was all gangbusters about wanting to be on the show; he couldn't have been more enthusiastic. Now, I was pretty enthusiastic about the stock at the time too, so when he came on the show, I made sure to be extra hard on the guy in order to temper my enthusiasm.

When I brought Greehey on the show, he told me, and all of you, that his stock was cheap. I, in my own charming way, told him talk was cheap. I wanted to hear something more substantive before I gave his stock my seal of approval. And he gave it to me. He told me I was exactly right, which is why he was going to try to buy back every single share that his company could legally purchase. When you get a CEO who's so confident his stock is cheap that he's willing to tell you that his company will be a huge buyer, that's when you know you've got a winner on your hands. After he said this, I went running to the BUY BUY BUY button, because, man, he meant that his stock was cheap. So how'd that interview work for you if you listened to me and to the CEO of Valero? If you bought the stock where I recommended it after the interview on May 18, 2005, at sixty-three smackers and change, you caught a double in Valero by January 30, 2006. If you're more of a short-term investor, I should point out that by the end of August, the stock had broken through a hundred. I feel great about that double because I'd emphasized that I couldn't be more effusive in my endorsement of the company. I was enthusiastic before I brought the CEO on, but the interview took that enthusiasm to a whole new level and I hope helped some people make a lot of money. That's what a Cramer-seal-of-approval interview looks like: I'm already positive about a stock, and the CEO comes on, reassures me, and says something to make me even more positive. That's a green light for you to buy, and as you see from this example, it can make you a lot of money.

There are some other great ways you can tell that you should buy a stock from a CEO interview. When a CEO comes on the show and it's clearly against his own interest to come on, that really means something. What does that look like? The best example I can think of is the interview I did with Les Moonves, the incredibly cool CEO of CBS. He came on the show the same day that CBS was launched as a separate entity from Viacom, its former parent company. This was clearly not in his interest, because CNBC, the network *Mad Money* is on, competes with his television network. And while we're talking about conflicts of interest, I should mention that CBS is the parent company of Simon & Schuster, the publisher of this book, and of CBS Radio, where the *Real Money* radio show runs. I'm not praising Les Moonves because, in a way, I work for him. You know me better than that. The point here isn't even that he's a cool CEO; I'm just using CBS to illustrate a broader example. Moonves was really taking a chance by coming on my show. I emphasized this fact when he came on, and I also told him I was skeptical of his company's ability to grow. Remember, when I bring these CEOs on, I want to make them address substantive problems with their companies. Moonves told me that he knew he was taking a chance, but it was a chance worth taking. The analysts, he said, were underrating his stock, and people didn't understand how great the story behind CBS really was. Les Moonves came on with total enthusiasm in the face of a hostile network, and he had me sold. I liked this interview so much that I told people to buy the stock, and what do you know, it went higher. The lesson here is simple: if a CEO has something to lose by coming on *Mad Money,* he probably has a really great stock to pitch. That's another example of what a Cramer-seal-of-approval interview looks like.

I'm going to give you one more example of what it looks like when I bring on a CEO because I *already* like his stock. I can't stress the importance of recognizing these interviews enough, because they're almost always great signs that you should buy the stock. When I took

Mad Money on the road to Columbia University, I brought on George David, the CEO of United Technologies (UTX). I was already positive about the stock, but I had some concerns. United Technologies is generally considered a cyclical company, a company that's sensitive to rate hikes from the Federal Reserve. The CEO of United Technologies came out and told me several things. He said the stock was cheap; he said he intended to buy back as much of it as he could, which means he *really* meant it was cheap; he said his company had great earnings visibility; and he had total confidence in all five of its major business lines. A lot of CEOs will come on the show and tell me that their business is great, but not all of them will put their money where their mouth is and promise to buy back stock hand over fist. Then he gave me the real kicker. He said United Technologies had become largely an international company that wasn't hostage to the Federal Reserve. At the time, the Fed was raising rates. If you hadn't watched this interview you might have sold United Technologies. But as it turned out, UTX was one of a handful of industrial companies to perform very well as rates increased and the U.S. economy headed into a recession. After I heard all that, I became even more positive about the stock and told you to buy. The picture here is the same as before: if I like a stock before I bring a CEO on, and he actually makes me like the stock more, that's a real signal for you to buy it. The stock went much higher after the interview and made my charitable trust, Action Alerts PLUS, thousands of dollars.

The second reason I bring a CEO on the show is either to give him a chance to talk me out of a negative view I have of a stock or to respond to criticism that someone else has made. These interviews can also be great signals for you to buy the stock, but only if the CEO handles them correctly. If I have a negative view of a stock, it's usually very difficult to talk me out of that view. I'm all about flexibility, but my opinions are very well informed, and there's not a lot a CEO can say to get me to change my mind. When I do change my mind, that's very significant news for you. I'll give you another example to show you what this looks like. I brought on James Jenness, the terrific CEO of Kellogg (K), when I had a pretty unfavorable opinion of the stock. I didn't like it because its raw costs were coming up, and as a cereal maker, Kellogg really can't pass those costs along to its customers. But Jenness came on the show and told me that he had raw costs under control. He reassured me, and I changed my mind. What happened next? The stock went higher, and you made money if you were paying attention. The same thing happened when I brought on David Jaffe, the straight-shooting CEO of Dress Barn (DBRN). I didn't like Dress Barn stock because I didn't like any of the Dress Barn stores I'd gone to. Jaffe insisted I was wrong about the stock, and I went out of my way to give him a triple-buy because he was so convincing. Then the stock doubled. The point is clear: if a CEO can switch my opinion from a sell to a buy, or even a triple-buy, if he can take me from negative to incredibly enthusiastic, that's a stock that will probably make you a lot of money.

When I bring on a CEO to respond to criticism from another quarter, usually some analyst who doesn't like a stock, you can tell a lot about a company from the CEO's reaction. Sometimes executives will just dismiss negative research out of hand. That's OK, but you can't really learn anything from it. What I really like, and what really makes you money, is when a CEO comes on and patiently explains why the analysts are wrong about the stock. You want a CEO who will refute someone else's negative opinion point by point. That's a CEO I can get behind. The perfect example of this was when I brought on Michael Ward, the CEO of CSX (CSX), one of the few big railroad stocks. CSX had gone into free fall after what had looked like a great quarter. Ward came on and refuted all the negativity point by point. After the interview, I told people to let the stock come down more because the negativity was relentless, but then to buy it because management obviously had things under control. I probably wouldn't have told people to buy if Michael Ward hadn't been so patient and methodical about addressing the criticism of his company. The strategy made you 20 percent in five months.

Another good example of a CEO who responded the right way to negative information is Michael Watford, the CEO of Ultra Petroleum (UPL). I liked Ultra, but then the CFO left the company for reasons that weren't quite clear to me. It's one of my rules that when high-level people quit a company, you should become very suspicious. Think about the key departures at Enron before the bad numbers hit the fan. And when a CFO leaves, that's the worst. But Watford, the CEO, explained that the CFO really just wanted to take a break and that there was nothing to worry about. Now, this was a tough situation, because any smart CEO would say that no matter what. I told Watford that if he bagged my viewers, and he bagged me, I would be pretty upset with him, and I'd let everybody know. He rose to the challenge, so I told people to BUY BUY BUY, and then buyers caught a triple! If a CEO is willing to put his butt on the line to refute some criticism or negative piece of information, that really gives me confidence in the stock, and it should give you confidence, too.

I want to throw some more examples at you, because if I were reading this chapter, I'd be skeptical. I'd think it were possible that I'm just credulous and lucky. But I'm telling you, luck's got nothing to do with it. Take Countrywide Financial (CFC). The stock hit a fifty-two-week low after a series of downgrades, and I was negative about it too because it was a mortgage company and those tend to do poorly in the middle of a Fed-mandated economic slowdown, which is where we were in the business cycle. The CEO of Countrywide, Angelo Mozilo, actually called me to try to get on the show to explain the great story behind his stock. He came on and patiently explained that the analysts who covered his stock didn't understand the service stream of his business. He walked me through his business model, openly questioned the homework ethic of the analysts covering his stock, and convinced me that Countrywide was a triple-buy. Then the stock rose 30 percent. So you see, when a CEO is willing to refute the negativity point by point, and when he does it well, there are real opportunities for you to make money. The same thing happened when Jim Konrath, the fantastic and open CEO of Accredited Home Lenders (LEND)—how can you not love that stock symbol?—came on to refute a *Wall Street Journal* article about how his subprime lending business could be in trouble in a Fed-induced slowdown. He convinced me—and I hope you—that people were too negative at the bottom, and you caught a terrific 15-point move on the backs of the short sellers. (It later came back down, but it was a great trade!)

I believe in proof, I believe in rigor, so I want to throw some more examples at you. People are too ready to write off my CEO interviews as a part of the show that makes no money, but I've got clear evidence to the contrary. So here's another example: Celgene (CELG). Celgene had pulled out of a Bear Stearns health-care conference, and that caused the stock to plummet. That sort of thing usually raises a lot of eyebrows. It makes people wonder what the company is so afraid of, and that makes people sell. So Bob Hugin, the president of Celgene, and also a neighbor of mine whose daughter played soccer with my daughter, called me up to say that it was all a big mistake. Celgene pulled out of the conference because of a transportation snafu. I invited him on the show the next day, where he repeated what he'd told me. I gave Celgene a buy. If you listened, you could've caught a double.

There's a third way watching these interviews can make you money: when a CEO comes on my show and exudes a kind of tempered confidence when his stock is down, I tend to like that. It's reassuring because it lets you know that the company's management knows what it's doing and isn't wildly overoptimistic or even dishonest. The best example of this was my interview with Fred Hassan, turnaround expert and CEO of Schering-Plough (SGP). I was very enthusiastic about his stock, which I thought was a great turnaround story. But he, straight shooter that he is, told me that the turnaround would take longer than he'd like. He dampened my enthusiasm for the turnaround, but made me like the company even more. Hassan wanted to be sure that I and all my viewers understood that the company had a lot more problems than he had realized when he took over. What does it mean when a CEO says that things will be good, but they aren't good yet? It means he wants only patient people in the stock. He's not looking for growth guys; he's looking for long-term value investors. This kind of honesty is very encouraging. It led me to tell people to buy Schering-Plough, but to be patient with it; sure enough, if you did that you would've caught a 20 percent move higher. It didn't happen at once, it took about a year, but 20 percent in a year is a pretty good return. Now, Hassan's my neighbor in New Jersey, so you could expect he wouldn't bag me, or bag you on the show. But remember, it's not just the fact that I'm friends with these guys that keeps them honest. You know I'm not about making friends; I'm about trying to make you money. One of the great things I can do is make CEOs tell me the truth, because they know they'll look bad if they mislead me or my viewers.

The fourth way my CEO interviews can make you money is rare, but when it happens, you better take notice. There are occasions when I'll bring on a CEO and he'll hint at something incredibly newsworthy. It can't really be news, because if it were, that would be illegal. But a CEO or a CFO can certainly hint at certain kinds of things that can make you money. Once again, let me give you an example and then break it apart to show you how this kind of thing works. Back on July 25, 2006, I brought on the CEO of Nabors Industries (NBR), Eugene Isenberg. Nabors is a driller of oil and natural gas. When I brought its CEO on, the stock had been taking a beating. It was the cheapest driller out there because it had a lot of natural gas exposure, and at the time, natural gas had gotten very cheap. When I say cheap, I mean cheap relative to where it had been the year before, not according to historical standards. You'd never think natural gas was cheap looking at your heating bill, but the previous year the commodity had been trading more than twice as high. The actual price of natural gas has very little to do with the price a company like Nabors gets for the use of one of its drilling rigs. Nabors' earnings are determined by supply and demand in the rig market—by the number of rigs out there—not by the spot price of natural gas. There weren't many rigs, so Nabors' stock should've been doing very well. But because most people didn't understand what the business was actually levered to, the stock had been beaten day after day after day. This was all the worse for me because I owned it for my charitable trust at the time.

(I've mentioned my charitable trust a couple of times so far in the book. It's a small pool of money that I manage as part of a subscription service at www.ActionAlertsPLUS.com. I manage this money with a lot of restrictions. If I mention a stock on television or radio, I can't touch it in Action Alerts for five days. I must hold every stock for at least a month, and I can't short stocks or use options. Every time I'm about to make a trade, I send out an e-mail to the subscribers explaining what I'm going to do and why. And I send out tons of more important e-mails about what *I would* do if I didn't have the restrictions. I make no money on the gains in the stocks that I hold in the Action Alerts PLUS portfolio. Instead, the profits go to certain charities that I designate—for example, the Imus Ranch; the Boys and Girls Club of Baton Rouge, Louisiana (post-Katrina); and the Fallen Heroes Fund. The money I raise from the subscriptions goes to TheStreet. com, which hosts the Action Alerts PLUS Web site, and as a shareholder in TheStreet.com I do make money on the subscriptions.)

But let's get back to the point. I brought on the CEO of Nabors at a time when the stock was near its fifty-two-week low, even though I felt it deserved to be much higher. I asked the CEO if he would be willing to take the company private if the stock didn't start getting more respect. Now obviously the CEO of a publicly held company can't just come on TV and say "Yes, I will take the company private if the stock doesn't start going higher soon." That's the kind of information that has to be disclosed in a press release. Even though Gene Isenberg couldn't say that to me on air, he could hint at it. He told me that the company was already buying back stock, which in effect was slowly taking the company private over time, and that if Nabors continued to be cheap, he'd consider taking it totally private.

It sounds as though Gene Isenberg was equivocating. But remember, these guys can't break news, and if they lie, they could get in a lot of trouble. That's why you have to watch for hints like the one I just described. I know he didn't say it explicitly, but the takeaway from that interview was that if Nabors stayed cheap, it would either sell itself to a private equity firm or take itself private. If you own a stock and the company it's loosely associated with gets taken private, it's usually being taken private at a premium, which means you stand to make a lot of money. So the takeaway from an interview where a CEO hints that if his stock stays cheap, he'll possibly take the company private, is that you should buy the stock. Nabors then reported a great quarter and drove 15 percent higher before filling back with oil later in the year.

These kinds of hints are actually more common than you might expect. They usually come out when I ask a CEO or a CFO what he intends to do about something. If a company is sitting on a lot of cash, you can bet I'll ask him what he'll do with it. A CEO or CFO can't really tell me what he is going to do with the cash unless he has already announced it to the public. That means my question is more about gauging the intensity of the response; it's about reading the way a CEO says something. Think of listening for hints in a CEO interview as being similar to reading poetry. I doubt very many of you read poetry. But if I ask a CEO what he's going to do with his billion dollars of cash and he says they've talked about doing a buyback, or paying a dividend, or expanding their operations, then you don't have to leave it at that. The way the CEO talks about these different strategic alternatives will be different. If it sounds like he really favors that dividend, then I wouldn't necessarily bet money on it, but

I would assume the dividend would be more likely than the other two alternatives.

Remember, if it's useful information, a CEO can't just come out and say it. And the flip side of that is that you can't rely too heavily on the hints you try to sift out of these interviews. However, hints can be useful; they are worth listening to; and they've made me money in the past. You just have to follow my advice in this chapter so you know what's worth listening to and what to tune out whenever I interview a CEO or a CFO.

Those are the ways watching my CEO interviews can make you money. But the interviews are also incredibly valuable because they can help you not lose money. Not losing money is at least half of investing well. As long as you know what to look for you can save yourself a lot of money and a lot of heartbreak, maybe a lot of hair loss too—although I won't vouch for that. There are five ways a CEO interview can help you avoid owning a real loser of a stock.

The first way an interview can help you not lose money is when a CEO can't back up my own optimism about his stock. When I did the show at Columbia, I didn't just interview the CEO of United Technologies, I also brought on Ray Milchovich, the CEO of Foster Wheeler (FWLT). This is a great example of an interview that could've saved you a lot of pain. At the time I brought Milchovich on, I owned the stock for my charitable trust. I wanted to hear that the company was doing really well because it was at its fifty-two-week high, and any stock at its fifty-two-week high had better be doing well. I wanted to hear that Foster Wheeler, with a clean balance sheet after years of being mired in debt, was ready to do a buyback. Even though the stock was flying high, it had been the victim of multiple bear raids, and I was hoping the CEO could give shareholders some stability in the way the stock was being traded. I'll give Milchovich credit for being honest. He didn't reassure me about the stock deserving to be on that fifty-two-week high list, and he didn't give me any assurance about the buyback. He also claimed he had no idea what I was talking about when I asked him about the terrible way the stock traded. That led me to give Foster Wheeler a clear don't buy. I lightened up on the stock for my charitable trust, and if you were watching the show, it would've been clear that I was unhappy with this interview and that Foster Wheeler was a stock to avoid. What happened? It went down 20 straight points. So if you sold, I saved you a lot of money. If I have concerns about a stock and they don't get addressed, if a CEO doesn't tell me what I want to hear, that's a stock you probably want to sell.

Sometimes—and you'll mostly see this with CFOs because they're more familiar with the numbers and less promotional than CEOs—you'll get a guy who comes on and just tells you the stock is bad. This is the second way a CEO interview can save you money—I call it the honest-man factor. I have enormous respect for anyone who does this, and I think it gives an executive a lot of credibility. I once brought on Charles Kleman, the CFO of Chico's FAS (CHS), a clothing re-tailer that I really liked at the time. I read him a piece of negative research about the stock, expecting that he'd refute it. But out of no-where he actually agreed with the negative research. That kind of honesty is stunning, and it can really save you a lot of money. Because of Kleman's honesty, I was able to give Chico's a triple-sell before the stock got cut in half. Whenever a CFO is cautious, I'm cautious. If a CFO is negative, I'm negative. You can take that as gospel.

There are some less-becoming ways you can tell that a company is a sell when I bring on its CEO. If I bring on a CEO and we start to get testy with each other, you ought to be very, very cautious about the stock. This is the third way my CEO interviews can save you money. I'll give you two examples here. The CEO of Toll Brothers (TOL) Bob Toll, and Bill Zollars, the CEO of Yellow Roadway—which now trades under a different name, YRC Worldwide (YRCW)—both cre-ated this kind of triple-sell situation. Both of these guys insisted that their companies could totally buck any type of economic slowdown. Now I've been in this business for a long time, and I know for a fact that neither a homebuilder like Toll Brothers nor a shipping company like Yellow Roadway can do well in a slowdown. I told these guys that I thought they were wrong, but they stuck to their guns. I would have liked both stocks a lot more if Bob Toll and Bill Zollars had just admitted that things could go badly. The fact that they didn't admit that led me to tell people to sell both stocks. It was clear that they weren't preparing themselves for trouble—they were too cocky. Both of them were way too defensive about their business; they were way too unwilling to admit to potential problems. That's never a good sign. Whenever I see that, I'm going to give you an immediate sell. If you catch this kind of interchange, now you'll know to sell before I even hit the button. Both these stocks, by the way, went down horribly after my interviews with their CEOs, so again, you can be sure that what I'm telling you actually works.

If a CEO ducks a really tough question on the show, you should be ready to sell the stock. That's the fourth thing you should watch for if you're trying to avoid losing money. What does this look like? I brought on Steve Sanghi, the CEO of Microchip (MCHP). He's usually a straightforward guy, and Microchip is a great company that makes a lot of the guts of all the gadgets we use and love. But Sanghi just wouldn't answer or even address my suggestion that there might be a glut of big-screen TVs. When you see a CEO, especially one who's usually very straightforward, do that kind of thing, you'd better be cautious. I took that interview as a warning, not just about Microchip, but also about every other company that was depending on big-screen TVs to make money. If there's an inventory glut of a product, that usually means you're going to see a shortfall from anyone who makes that product. This interview with the Microchip CEO made me wonder aloud about Corning (GLW) and Best Buy (BBY). Both of these stocks later got hit because of that big-screen TV glut. When you see a dodged question, you can save yourself a lot of money as long as you take swift action.

There's one more way these interviews can keep you from losing money. As I mentioned earlier, I can use my media presence to keep

CEOs honest. A while back I brought on David Aldrich, the CEO of Skyworks Solutions (SWKS). I made it very clear that I could embarrass him in multiple media venues if he was too bullish and bagged my viewers. That made him really temper his enthusiasm, and it kept you out of a stock that turned out to be a pretty poor performer.

I don't want to make it sound like I always get these interviews right. I don't always nail it. You should keep this in mind. You must always be a skeptic if you want to be a good investor, and that includes being skeptical of me. If a CEO gets his stock wrong, then I'm gonna get it wrong too. When I went to the University of Michigan I brought on the CEO of Domino's Pizza (DPZ), a guy named David Brandon. I was skeptical about the stock, but Brandon assured me that all was well. I foolishly got converted by the moment. I had an enthusiastic crowd of college students and a strong-sounding CEO. I went positive on the stock. Their same-store sales had a downturn shortly after and I ended up hurting people. I'm far from flawless—ask anyone who knows me—and I'm not always right about stocks. You need to be right only about 60 percent of the time to do really well, but I want to make sure you don't put too much faith in my ability to interview CEOs, because I hate it when you get hurt, even just partially, because of my show.

There's one more aspect of these CEO interviews that I want to touch on. Most CEOs are polite, statesmanlike guys. They almost never criticize their competitors. So if you ever see a CEO criticizing one of his competitors on my show, you'd better start listening closely. One time I brought on Tom Stemberg, the man who built Staples (SPLS)—he's a retired CEO for whom I have a lot of respect. He said he had some worries about Wal-Mart (WMT), which, at the time, had just inched toward its fifty-two-week high. Stemberg told me the model was having problems overseas, and he predicted that Wal-Mart would have to retreat from Germany. Obviously that would hurt the stock. I was really shocked by this, because as I said, CEOs almost never criticize other companies. I decided there must be something really wrong with Wal-Mart and told people to sell. Sure enough, Wal-Mart pulled out of Germany, and the stock fell by 20 percent.

Now you know how I approach my CEO interviews, and you know the thought process that goes into my recommendations after I get through with an executive. I'll tell you what I think you should do with a stock after I finish the interview on the show, so you don't have to do a lot of thinking. But I want to teach you, not just hand-feed you stocks. Some of these rules for watching my CEO interviews will apply any time you see a CEO on television. If you see him being evasive or criticizing another company or getting testy, those are all things to watch out for. If you see a CEO, even on some show that isn't *Mad Money,* patiently and methodically refuting someone's negative opinions on his stock, you know that's a good sign. Now that you know how to read management, you should be able to turn my interviews into money in your pocket.

8

NEW MISTAKES, NEW RULES

Ten Lessons from My Bad Calls

I approach *Mad Money* with more rigor, hard work, and intensity than I ever did at my hedge fund, and when I was running money there, I tried to be the hardest-working man on Wall Street. When I screwed up at Cramer Berkowitz, my hedge fund, I hurt only a small group of wealthy investors, and only a handful of people, all my employees, knew about it. When I make a mistake on *Mad Money,* not only do hundreds of thousands, if not millions, of people know about it, but a lot more people, not all of them incredibly wealthy, stand to get hurt. In other words, the stakes are much higher on *Mad Money* than they ever were at the hedge fund, even though I don't have any of my money on the line. I have something much more important riding on every show: my reputation.

That's why when I make a mistake on *Mad Money,* I can't write it off. I can't do what I did at my hedge fund, where I had a closet of boxes full of paper with all my bad trades on them that I would pore over endlessly. I would beat myself up over the losing trades and try to figure out what I'd done wrong, so I could avoid doing it again in the future. On *Mad Money,* even that isn't enough because it's your money on the line, not the money of thirty-eight really rich families. I wrote my last book, *Jim Cramer's Real Money: Sane Investing in an Insane World,* before I had *Mad Money,* and even though that book remains very useful, it's not the be-all and end-all of investment advice. As I've said earlier, I have learned more about investing in a year of *Mad Money* than I learned in five years at my hedge fund. That's because *Mad Money* is harder work than the hedge fund: I need to generate more new, good ideas than I ever had to while running money, and I'm in a much more perilous position on the show, so I have to work a lot harder.

Just as at the fund, I learned my best lessons on the show from getting stocks wrong, really wrong. Because I approach the show like registering a piece of artillery—I use my misses to recalibrate, find the right target eventually, and hit a bull's-eye—I've learned from those mistakes and made the show better. That's good for you because it makes *Mad Money* a more valuable, better-tuned resource. But it's not enough that *I* learn from my mistakes on the show. I want *you* to learn from them too. Let my pain and public humiliation be your gain. It's better for you to watch me make a bonehead mistake on the show and embarrass myself than to make that mistake with your own money. You can and should learn from your own mistakes, but why repeat my errors if you don't have to? Why lose a single extra penny if you can avoid it? And I still wear the Post-it on my forehead when I screw up, except this time it's on national TV!

In *Real Money,* I gave you a list of rules that I'd put together to stop myself from making mistakes at my hedge fund. Those rules still apply, but they're not enough. The world has changed in the last two years, and I've learned a lot more about investing. That's why I have ten new rules, culled from my worst mistakes on *Mad Money.* These are new rules for a new time. My last set of rules was designed to help ordinary investors deal with the market. Since starting *Mad Money*, I've realized that "the market" is an unsophisticated, unhelpful way of approaching your investments. That's why both the show and the rules I've created in response to my mistakes on the show aren't about "the market." They're about the big institutions, the hedge funds and the mutual funds, that dominate "the market." It's these institutions that set prices, because they do most of the buying and selling. As an individual investor, you are dwarfed by these institutions, and you need to know how to respond to them and how to anticipate their moves if you want to make a lot of money. With these rules, you won't feel or be helpless in the face of the behemoths who whip around your stocks. My ten new rules, coming out of hard-earned lessons on *Mad Money*, will help you—the small, individual investor—beat the big institutions at their own game. That's the secret now: not just looking at "the market" as an abstract force, but looking at the big institutions that make up the market and anticipating their every move. If you listen to my new rules, and if you watch *Mad Money*, you'll be able to compete with and defeat the big institutions and make yourself a lot of money. Sane investing in an insane world isn't enough anymore: the market's gotten harder. You need to be a madman to make money in this market, and that's why I'm here to help you get inside the head of the craziest man on Wall Street.

Here are your new rules, the ten lessons I've learned from my most embarrassing moments on *Mad Money*. Read and learn about the new shape of the market so you can stop crying and start making money with my new disciplines. Most blooper reels just try to make you laugh; with this one, I'm trying to make you money.

1. Resisting the business cycle is futile. It doesn't matter how much you like a stock based on the fundamentals, it doesn't even matter what a stock's "real" relationship to the business cycle is, if you buy a secular growth stock when we're in a cyclical upturn, or a supposedly cyclical stock when we're in an economic slowdown, you will lose. I

wish this weren't true. I wish Wall Street were smart and had discerning taste, but that's not how the game works. The mutual funds and the hedge funds are the only players who count, and it's their opinions that determine where a stock goes. The big institutions all obey the cycle. They're the reason I drew up my chart about cyclical investing. And if they obey the cycle, then stocks will obey the cycle, too. The big institutional investors sell secular growth stocks when the economy is strong, and they sell cyclicals when the economy is weak. End of story. If you try to fight this, if you tell yourself that your stock is so good the cycle can't hurt it, if you believe a stock isn't cyclical when the Street thinks it is, you'll lose. Sometimes you just have to bite the bullet, acknowledge that these big funds aren't that smart, accept that they're captive to their own rules, and sell a really good stock because the cycle has turned against it.

I learned this lesson the hard way in UnitedHealth Group, (UNH). I'd liked this stock well before *Mad Money* premiered on March 15, 2005, and owned it for my charitable trust. At the beginning of the show, the stock was a split-adjusted forty-five bucks a share. I made so much money in the stock and liked it so much that I was calling myself Dr. UNH. If you listened to me and bought UNH in the forties, you could've ridden the stock up to its peak, well over sixty smackers a share in December 2005. And if you kept listening to me, you rode it back down to the low forties. My biggest mistake in this stock was that I tried to resist the cycle. I had been extremely positive on UNH during a period where the Fed was raising rates and the economy seemed slow. UNH is a health-care stock, maybe *the* health-care stock of health-care stocks. That means it has a place on the cycle: it's a secular growth play. You own it when the Fed is raising rates and the economy is weak. If you obey the cycle, you also have to sell it when the economy starts to turn around.

In the first half of 2006, the economy started to turn around. In the first quarter, we had 5.6 percent economic growth—that's incredible growth, the sign of a healthy economy. Right up until the May

2006 Fed meeting, we were in a noticeable cyclical upturn. That meant all the big funds were selling their shares of UNH to buy shares of more cyclical companies like Caterpillar or Ingersoll-Rand. I kept telling people to hang on to their UNH in spite of the sector rotation out of health-care stocks and into cyclicals, but that was a mistake. If you'd sold UNH near the top, after it was apparent the cycle was turning and conventional manufacturing business was getting stronger, but well before the stock bottomed in the low forties, you could have saved yourself 20 straight points of pain. (The market switched in May when the Fed braked too hard; the market fled the cyclicals and came back to the HMOs.)

If you learn from the mistake I made here, you won't repeat it yourself. I was insistent that even though there was a serious rotation out of the health-care stocks into the deep cyclicals—mining, minerals, smelting, and the like—the fundamentals at UNH, that is, their earnings and their great management team, justified holding on to the stock. I kept telling people that if you'd bought UNH on weakness any time in the last ten years, you made money. Rotations come and go, I said, but the fundamentals ultimately win out, and the fundamentals at UNH were great. I was wrong. I tried to fight the cycle with the fundamentals, but the fund managers don't care about the fundamentals as much as they care about the cycle. It simply was not worth sitting through a 25 or 30 percent decline in UNH's stock price.

As I learned, and as you should learn, the right thing to do in this situation is sell the stock. Even when you like the stock's fundamentals, even when it's already made you a lot of money, you don't want to fight the cycle. We know buy and hold doesn't work, but neither will buy and homework if you don't take the business cycle and sector rotations into account. I should have sold. Then, when the economy inevitably slowed down again and health-care stocks came back into favor, I should have told you to get back into UNH. I should have been a matador and gotten out of the way of the bull that was the cycle. I have taken this lesson to heart on the show, and I no longer try to fight the cycle. Even if the big hedge funds and mutual funds that sell these stocks because of where we are in the cycle are "wrong," they're still going to knock the stocks down, and who wants to lose money when you don't have to?

It doesn't even matter if the big institutions misbrand a stock as secular or cyclical. The only thing that counts is their perception. Often they'll get it wrong, but if they get it wrong, there's nothing you can do about it, and you shouldn't try to fight them. I'd rather make money than be right, to butcher one of Henry Clay's greatest lines. Take what happened with CSX, the big railroad company. On July 25, 2006, I tried to convince my viewers and Wall Street that CSX, even though historically thought of as a cyclical stock, wasn't actually cyclical. I diligently went through the kinds of goods CSX transports and pointed out that most of that stuff wasn't cyclical in nature. That meant CSX couldn't really be considered a cyclical stock. It didn't matter. As far as the big institutions were concerned, CSX was a railroad, and railroads are cyclical. Since the economy seemed to be staring a recession right in the face at the time, the big funds were selling off everything cyclical left and right, even if, when you gave it a good hard look, the stocks weren't actually cyclical. These big institutional players don't give stocks a good hard look. They're creatures of instinct and reflex, like reptiles. When I told you to buy CSX, I thought I looked really smart because I was pointing out a big mistake the Street was making, but the Street kept making the mistake, and you didn't make money. You lost 7 points overnight! (Michael Ward, the CEO, did a good job defending the stock on my show, as I said in the last chapter, but you got hurt before he came on.)

If you really like a stock that the Street thinks is out of favor in the cycle, wait for better opportunity to buy it, when it's more in favor and it's more likely to get bought by the big players and go up. When I fought the cycle in UNH and CSX, I lost. I'm not going to repeat that mistake. On the show I say that when you go to the dentist to get a cavity filled you don't even think twice, you take the Novocain. That's stepping aside, selling, letting the stock drop, and then picking it up after the pain. Don't fight the cycle. Don't repeat my mistake, because it'll cost you.

2. There's a market for everything; pay attention to it. It's tempting to treat stocks as pieces of paper that represent shares of companies. But that's not how it works. Stocks are pieces of paper that get traded in a market and valued by different investors for different reasons. There are different markets for different kinds of stocks. If you ignore this fact, you're setting yourself up for failure. If the market gets flooded with a certain type of stock, let's say Internet stocks, then the value of all those stocks will go down. That's what happened in 2000. We had too many dot-com IPOs, and there was only so much demand for dot-com stocks. That demand is created by the big funds, and it's always finite. The fund managers want only so many shares of dot-com companies, or any other kind of company. You need to pay attention to the fact that there's a market for Internet stocks, a market for commodity stocks, a market for drug stocks, a market for tech stocks, and so on. If the market gets flooded with supply, then just as in Economics 101, the price of everything on the market goes down. By the same token, if supply dries up, say if half the companies in an industry get taken private, then the price of everything else in the industry should go up. If you ignore this fact about the nature of the market, you'll get burned.

I coined this rule after I was publicly humiliated by the Sealy (ZZ) initial public offering, on April 7, 2006. There's a market for IPOs, a market for newly public stocks, and if you're going to try to invest in an IPO, you have to watch the supply and demand in that market. This is just as important as the stock's fundamentals. I really liked the Sealy company. I liked the road show put on by management in the weeks and months leading up to its IPO, and I told people to buy the stock. I recommended buying it up to $18 a share, based on both the company's fundamentals and what I perceived as the high demand for Sealy stock. As it turned out, the stock peaked at $18.20 and sank for weeks after, until it bottomed at about $12 two months later, in June. Why did I think there would be a lot of demand for Sealy? In that same quarter, there had been tremendous demand for stock in the Under Armour IPO, the Tim Hortons IPO, and the iRobot IPO. I got all those stocks right, by the way, but that didn't translate into getting Sealy right. I thought that because there had been a lot of demand for stock in these previous IPOs, the same would hold true for Sealy. In fact, the exact opposite was true. There was a finite amount of demand for newly public companies, for shares in these IPOs, and by the time Sealy came public, a lot of that demand had already been satisfied. There were just too many deals going on at that moment. The quarter Sealy came public had seen the most IPOs since the dot-com flood. That meant that there was a glut of newly public stocks on the market, and that it translated into Sealy fetching a lower price than I expected, because there weren't as many institutional buyers. The institutions had already gotten in on the IPOs that they wanted. They were all IPOed out.

If I'd paid attention to the IPO market, to the fact that there had been so many deals already that quarter, I would've been a lot less bullish about Sealy. There was too much IPO supply, and even if there were more demand than ever, that oversupply would still have been a bad sign for Sealy. There's a market for everything, and if you ignore that market, you'll miss some very important factors that determine a stock's price. As it happened, Sealy was also the lowest-quality IPO of the quarter, the worst-of-breed new stock to hit the market. When you're looking at the supply and demand for different types of stock, you should also pay attention to the quality of the stocks in that market. If there is a glut, the lowest-quality stock in the group will get hit the hardest, and if there is a shortage, the highest-quality stock will make you the most money. There was a glut of IPOs in the second quarter of 2006, and Sealy was probably the lowest-quality IPO. I knew that at the time, because Sealy was coming public after it had been through a leveraged buyout, or LBO.

For anybody who missed the 1980s, a leveraged buyout means that one company borrows a bunch of money, buys another company, and uses the new company as collateral against the debt. Then the new owners pay off the debt with the profits from the company they just bought. Sealy had been bought by an LBO firm and was being sold by it. The IPO was all about making money for the leveraged buyout guys who owned the company. Remember this: you can't trust companies that are coming out of a leveraged buyout. The investment banks will promote the stocks to you, but the investment banks favor the LBO firms because they do a lot more business with them than they do with the average investor. The banker wants to get all the LBO firm's deals, so he lays you down on the tracks to get it biz. That's right, the investment bank just wants to make money from the stream of deals that comes from screwing you; the LBO outfit wants to make money selling you a stock for more than it's worth; and there's nobody out there looking out for your interests—nobody but you. I'm supposed to help, but I dropped the ball with Sealy. All the big institutional investors on Wall Street knew this about Sealy. They knew the IPO was just designed to make the leveraged buyout firm money—not you—and that the stock wasn't all that terrific. If Sealy had been the only big IPO that quarter, the stock might have done well. I might still have gotten it right. But because Sealy was the worst of a large number of IPOs, the institutions that might have wanted exposure to an IPO had already gotten their fill with better companies.

Now you've learned from my mistake, you know to pay attention to the separate markets for different types of stocks and look at them as questions of supply and demand, just as with any other commodity. If you keep this in mind, you won't get burned as I got burned by Sealy.

3. It's not enough to do the homework; you have to do the right homework. Different kinds of trades and investments call for different kinds of homework. I always tell you to do the homework, but what that means can depend on what you're trying to accomplish. There's nothing more dangerous than thinking you've done all the right homework only to find out later that you've been researching the wrong aspects of a company. If you're investing in a stock for eighteen months, you want to look at the company's fundamentals and make sure it's going to perform over that long period. If you're only going to be in the stock for a month, you're probably looking for a specific catalyst to drive the stock higher; in that case, you need to research everything about that catalyst and the company's relationship to it. If you're trying to make money overnight, it's not with my help, because *Mad Money* can't make you money overnight, and I don't try to do that on the show. But if you are trying to make that overnight money, then you're definitely betting on a single, specific catalyst, and you need to know everything you can about that catalyst. You don't really need to know about a company's long-term, two-to-three-year prospects if you're trying to make money overnight; you need to know about its immediate prospects. Learning about each of these things requires different kinds of homework. When you confuse them, you won't be making truly informed trading or investment decisions. That means you won't be making any money.

I had to create this rule for myself after I recommended Dick's Sporting Goods (DKS) on August 15, 2005. I made this company my stock of the week, I laid my credibility on the line for it, but I'd done the wrong kind of homework. When I recommended Dick's, it was reporting earnings the very next day. Now you know I always tell people to do their homework, never buy stocks after hours and always use limit orders. I also know that not many people listen to me when I explain those rules. I said that Dick's would have a great quarter, and I know that people rushed to buy the stock ahead of their announcement the next morning in an attempt to make a quick buck. On the fifteenth, the day I got behind the stock, Dick's closed at $39.23. After I recommended it, the stock spiked to well over $40 a share in after-hours trading. The next day, Dick's came out with its earnings. The company fell well short of expectations. The stock opened at $35 on the sixteenth, and it settled even farther down to close at $32.90. If you'd gotten in the stock at $40 after hours—and you probably would have had to pay closer to $41—and then if you'd held on to the stock until the close, you would have lost almost 18 percent in this investment overnight. Eighteen percent overnight is about as bad as it gets.

I recommended Dick's ahead of the quarter, but I hadn't done enough homework about the quarter. I'd done homework about Dick's longer-term fundamentals. I looked at the number of stores the company had; I evaluated Dick's as a regional-to-national retail story—the kind that can make you a lot of money because it's got a lot of growth, and Wall Street loves growth. And all that stuff matters; it's part of your homework on an investment. But it's not part of your homework on a catalyst-based trade, like betting on a company's earnings. If a company has an earnings shortfall, odds are good its stock will go down. You beat earnings, your stock goes up. As an investor, if you're trying to game an earnings report, you need to do homework only on the three months that the company is reporting on. Will their same-store sales, revenues, and earnings in those three months fall short of, meet, or beat expectations? Will the company do so well or so poorly in the quarter that it's forced to raise or lower its guidance for the rest of the year? Those are the questions you have to ask yourself if you're betting on an earnings report. You don't need to know about the store count. You don't have to estimate how many stores Dick's can build in how many states before it hits saturation and finishes growing. You don't need to know the company's long-term growth rate. You just need to know the facts about the quarter.

If I'd waited a day and recommended Dick's as a long-term investment after the stock cratered because of its disappointing quarter, then I would have done the right homework. You could even have made some money, because the stock did recover over the next year. But that's not what I did. I recommended Dick's the night before the quarter, in effect telling you to try to make money overnight. But I hadn't done the homework for *that* trade. You need to be careful to know what kind of homework you have to do for all your trades and investments, and to do that correct homework. Not all homework is the same. I made this mistake, and I was as publicly embarrassed as I've ever been. Laugh at me, but listen to this hard-won advice.

4. Latin America is always a trade. There are some parts of the world that are too politically and economically unstable ever to invest in, or at least that's what the big institutional buyers and sellers who set prices believe. You can make a lot of money in these emerging markets, but you're always trading, never investing. If you hold on to Latin American stocks for long enough, your gains will evaporate. These stocks will come up, but like clockwork, they'll go right back down. Maybe the cause is political instability, maybe it's left-wing governments that are a little too stable, maybe it's a rate hike by the Federal Reserve. I know you'd think that Latin American stocks wouldn't be sensitive to the Federal Reserve of the United States, but that's actually not true. Latin American stocks trade as if they're levered to the health of the U.S. economy, even when that isn't really the case at all. The real reason Latin America is always a trade has nothing to do with Latin America and everything to do with hedge funds and mutual funds in North America. Every big money manager who buys Latin American stocks is buying them as a trade. For all the reasons outlined above, the big institutional players actually hate to invest in Latin American stocks, and since these players set prices, you can't invest in Latin American stocks either. Sooner or later, the mutual fund and hedge fund money from America will pour out of these stocks and you'll be left holding significantly cheaper pieces of paper.

If the institutions won't invest, you can't invest either. You have to get out before they do, or you'll give up all your gains.

I don't want you to confuse this with investing in Brazil, Russia, India, and China, or BRIC, which I generally consider a good thing. When I talk about buying stocks with Brazilian exposure, I mean you should buy American or European companies that sell things to Brazil. I do not mean you should invest in Brazilian stocks, because those stocks fall under this rule. No matter how hot these stocks might be at the moment, the big fund managers treat them as pure trades, and they'll eventually sell en masse and knock the stocks down.

I had to write this rule after my experience with Bancolombia (CIB). I recommended Bancolombia at nineteen dollars and change on August 3, 2005, and I caught close to a double in the stock by March 2006. By June, it had traded back down to twenty-three dollars and change. Bancolombia was the biggest bank in Colombia, and so it was uniquely levered to the serious bull market in Latin America and to the Latin American credit revolution. For the first time, lots of people in Latin America were getting credit cards and mortgages. Most of you probably can't remember a time before credit cards in the United States, but they changed everything, and they made it possible for banks to make a lot of money. Bancolombia was making that money. There was a whole host of other Latin American stocks I liked: Banco Bradesco (BBD) in Brazil; América Móvil (AMX), the Latin American wireless provider; and more. All of them went up a lot. And then all of them came right back down.

The immediate catalyst for the most recent decline was the rate hike by the Federal Reserve on May 11, 2006, which sent all the emerging-market stocks plummeting. But that didn't really affect a Latin American bank like Bancolombia. It was just an excuse by the big players to take their profits. They were approaching Bancolombia and Latin America like a trade. They had an exit strategy. At one point, they all decided the trade was over and started bailing out of the stocks. But I didn't have an exit strategy. I kept recommending that people buy Bancolombia and its entire Latin American cohort all the way up, and I was still positive when the stocks cratered. I had lost sight of the fact that the big investors in these stocks didn't treat them like investments. They were all planning to take profits, and since most of the big institutions think alike, they were going to take profits at the same time, sending the stocks into free fall.

I know I've already told you about the importance of taking profits when you have them, of selling a stock when it's still up. I had made nearly twice my money in Bancolombia, and in that situation, I would ordinarily recommend that you take at least half your position off the table, so you're playing with the house's money. But in Latin American stocks, the rules are different, because big American institutional investors treat these stocks differently. When you have a big gain in a Latin American stock, you should take everything off the table, because that gain will evaporate before too long. That's what happened to me in Bancolombia. Don't let it happen to you.

Why am I singling out Latin America? Why not East Asia? Why not Russia? Why not Africa, which is both less developed and less politically stable than Latin America? The fact is, it's got nothing to do with Latin America. The fund managers are much more confident in East Asian countries as opportunities for investment. They've all but crowned China and India. Russia, though mind-bogglingly corrupt, is still given extra credit, probably because it's half in Europe and because of its enormous natural gas assets. No matter how corrupt a company like Gazprom becomes—Gazprom, by the way, is Russia's partially state-owned natural gas company—it still has the largest natural gas assets on earth. Most African stocks are natural resource plays: you have a lot of gold, silver, platinum, and diamonds. These stocks will thrive even in the midst of civil war. In fact, stocks with exposure to mining in Angola actually performed better during Angola's three-decades-long civil war than they have during the peace that followed. If Africa were developed enough to have publicly traded companies with exposure to its service or industrial sectors, then those would be permanent trades too, just like Latin America. But as it stands right now, this rule is pretty much exclusive to Latin American companies because that is the one region the institutional money managers think of as both uninvestable and totally tradable.

5. Don't be afraid to say it's too hard: some things like restaurant same-store sales, are just too difficult to game. There are hundreds of different ways to make money in the market, but not everything is worth betting on. There are some metrics that are just too hard to predict, and that means you shouldn't try to invest based on them. The hedge funds will try to game anything and everything, but that doesn't mean they have a method that works; it just means that they're willing to place big bets all over the place to try to make big money. But that makes everything in the market much more volatile than it used to be. From my experience on the show, the hardest metric to game, the one I think you should avoid trying to predict altogether, is same-store sales in the food-service business. There are hundreds of hedge funds that will try to figure out which way the same-store sales of restaurant stocks will go, and those funds will either buy large positions in the restaurant stocks or sell a lot of shares short depending on whether they're positive or negative about the numbers. This creates volatility. All the hedge fund guys who get it wrong will close out their positions, either by selling if the stock is down or by buying stock to cover their shorts if the stock is up. That makes betting on restaurant sales a dangerous game: you could make a lot of money or the stock could blow up in your face.

It's a dangerous game, and it's not one I think you can win. These numbers are just too hard for you, me, or anyone else to predict with any accuracy. You never want to go into a volatile situation without an edge, and when it comes to same-store sales at restaurants, believe me, no one has that edge. The risk is not worth taking. There are other, easier ways to make money. If you want to game same-store sales numbers, do it at a retailer, where you have a better shot at figuring out what the numbers will be ahead of time. If you want to invest in a restaurant stock, invest longer term so that you don't feel hostage to their same-store sales numbers every month. I came up with this rule, and have stuck to it, ever since I got totally bagged by Domino's Pizza (DPZ). As I mentioned in the previous chapter, I made my big mistake in this stock when I recommended it after interviewing the CEO, David Brandon, at the University of Michigan on April 25, 2006. The previous year, Domino's had delivered impressive same-store sales growth, which meant they would have an extra-difficult time maintaining or beating that level of growth in 2006. I made that point to the CEO, but he assured me that Domino's would be able to meet its same-store sales targets. I believed him, and I'm sure he was being totally honest. He just got it wrong. Shortly afterward, Domino's reported a same-store sales shortfall, and over the next three months the stock sank from $28, where it was when I recommended it at Michigan, down to $22.50.

Your lesson is not that I should have listened to myself and remained skeptical. When a CEO tells you he's going to deliver, he means it, and who knows more about a company than its CEO, other than the CFO? The lesson is much bigger and much more depressing than that. Sure I may have been right about Domino's initially, but my correct opinion wasn't based on a lot of homework. I knew Domino's was going to be up against tough compares, which means they were going to be measuring their growth against a really good previous year, but plenty of companies have gone up against tough compares before and won out. The real lesson here is that it's way too hard to figure out restaurant same-store sales. There are too many factors that go into producing those numbers, factors about consumer spending and eating habits that we just don't have much good information about as well as information about the success or failure of specific retail promotions. Even the CEO of Domino's, who should have known better than anyone, couldn't get it right. If even the Pizza Man can't game his own same-store sales, I can't think of a reason why anyone else should be able to. That's why I don't want you trying to invest in stocks based on this metric—it's too hard.

The problem extends beyond Domino's; it even extends beyond companies that get their same-store sales wrong. I've seen similar things happen at both Panera Bread (PNRA) and Starbucks (SBUX). Panera Bread had been one of the best regional-to-national growth stories in the restaurant business, and I'd been totally behind the company. But when they reported their second-quarter earnings on July 25, 2006, they also gave weak same-store sales guidance for the next month and for the rest of the year. The company also expanded the range of its expected full-year earnings downward, but it was the same-store sales guidance that killed the stock, which lost almost 12 percent of its value overnight. Panera thought it would do better, but because of a new product rollout, it had to knock down the forecasts. Panera had predicted that its new product would sell better and cost less than it did. When the results were in, they crushed the stock. Who could have predicted that? The same thing happened to Starbucks not long afterward when they changed their menu. Again—not predictable. Who would want to try to game that? These restaurants are just sitting ducks without much control over their own destiny. You can invest in them over the long term, but trying to game short-term metrics like same-store sales has only ever brought me a world of hurt.

In the case of Starbucks, the company reported a solid second quarter but disappointing July same-store sales on August 3, 2006. The stock, another one I'd been positive on, was down 8 percent by the close. Starbucks reported 4 percent same-store sales growth in July, when they'd given a pretty broad range of 3 to 7 percent growth. If they'd had 5.1 percent same-store sales growth, that would've been perceived as a beat, and the stock might have gone up. But there's no way for you to know whether Starbucks will report 4 percent, or 5 percent, or 6 percent, so I don't want you trying to invest in any of these stocks on the basis of the same-store sales numbers. I know from experience that you can't count on them and you can't predict them reliably. It's one of those metrics that's just too darn hard. There are countless other ways to make money investing. Stick with them and avoid the hard stuff. Howard Schultz, the great chairman of Starbucks, redeemed himself and his company the next month, but people got killed in the interim. Starbucks is worth sticking with as an investment because Schultz is so great and has a terrific long-term growth plan.

6. Not all companies that produce commodities are as interchangeable as their products. When you look over a group of oil producers, or copper producers, or nickel producers, or rock producers, you should have a natural tendency to think that all of the stocks are pretty much the same. They all do the same thing, and the product they produce is totally undifferentiated. After all, what's the difference between a ton of iron ore from one company and a ton of iron ore from another company? This kind of thinking is wrong. It's gotten me hurt in the past, and it could get you hurt in the future. Companies aren't just boxes that turn inputs into outputs and generate profits. Even commodity companies don't work that way. There are just too many ways for an oil company or a mineral company to screw up what should be an easy, profitable process. That's why you can't treat commodity companies like the commodities they produce, as interchangeable products. You have to differentiate between the good, the bad, and the ugly, even in business where you'd expect all companies to look pretty much the same. If you make the assumption that all oil and gas companies or all mineral companies are essentially the same, then you'll end up holding the worst ones and losing money hand over fist.

I had to set down this commandment after I got Energy Partners (EPL) dead wrong. I got behind Energy Partners on April 13, 2006, when it was trading at $24.35. Energy Partners is an oil and natural-gas exploration and production company, but it's tilted heavily toward exploring for new oil in the Gulf of Mexico. I said that Energy Partners was one of the cheapest exploration and production stocks out there. Because of its heavy exposure to the Gulf, Energy Partners had been beaten up by Hurricanes Katrina and Rita, which had hurt their business in the last quarter of 2005 and the first quarter of 2006. But Energy Partners had put the hurricanes behind them, or so I thought, and they were ready practically to print money finding new oil. Boy was I ever wrong. By June 13, just two months after I'd recommended the stock, it was bottoming at $17.67 a share, down well over 25 percent from where I'd initially backed the stock. Ultimately, if you hung out long enough, you made your money back when EPL got a takeover bid. But that's all you got. The bid came in right where I recommended it, so you got all the angst and none of the upside. I made the mistake of thinking that all companies that explore for and produce oil and natural gas were pretty much the same, that since they all produced the same stuff, there was no reason for Energy Partners to be so much cheaper than its peers.

When a stock is cheap, it's usually cheap for a reason. Energy Partners wasn't cheap just because Hurricane Katrina had done a lot of one-time damage to the company. It was cheap because it was a poorly run company that couldn't execute. Energy Partners did two things that really set it apart from other exploration and production companies; it gave you two reasons to stop treating all oil and gas companies as equals. First, on May 9, EPL came out with its second-quarter earnings. The company had a huge miss. The Street wanted 47¢, but Energy Partners gave them 37¢. Even though the consensus earnings estimates for Energy Partners were already low, EPL still missed. This was a clear case of underpromise, underdeliver. Energy Partners still hadn't recovered from Hurricane Katrina in the second quarter, and even though the Street expected some weakness from the hurricane, the company showed that it was really in shambles. Most other exploration and production companies with Gulf exposure had been able to recover, but not Energy Partners. This company couldn't execute. It couldn't put itself back together.

A good oil and gas company would have bounced back almost completely eight months after Katrina, but Energy Partners wasn't a good company, and the difference between good and bad here is the difference between making money and losing money. Then Energy Partners made another bonehead move. One of the reasons I'd recommended Energy Partners was that it was a small company that could be easily taken over by a much larger oil company. But the management of Energy Partners decided that rather than be taken over, they'd go and buy another company, Stone Energy, and pay way too much for it. Acquisitions usually drive down stocks, but pricey acquisitions can really hurt. That acquisition is a big part of why Energy Partners kept going down after its awful quarter. Bad management teams can hurt you by making bad decisions. Just because Energy Partners produced a totally undifferentiated product didn't make it the same as every other oil and gas company. If I had been more willing to believe that these companies were all different, and that there was a lot a bad management team could do to screw things up, I never would have recommended this stock.

I made the same mistake on July 21, 2006, although without the same disastrous results. I recommended both Vulcan Materials (VMC) and Martin Marietta Materials (MLM) as plays on highway spending because both companies make aggregate, the rocks you use to build roads. What could be more interchangeable than rocks, right? Once again, I was wrong. Although both stocks went up a lot within the next three weeks, Vulcan Materials went up 12 percent, Martin Marietta up 9 percent as of August 7. Vulcan went up more because it was a different company. It had rocks in California, and California was where most of the big highway spending was coming from. Even though these companies looked the same because they made the exact same product, they were still different, and that difference would have made or cost you money. When a company producers a commodity, its stock should not be traded or valued like a commodity. Even rocks can be different. Remember, sector analysis is 50 pecent of performance, not 100 percent. You need to look at more information about the specifics of a company before you equate it with its similar-looking competitors or you could get burned just as I did in Energy Partners.

7. Past performance is not an indicator of future success. If you make a lot of money in a sector or an industry, it's only natural for you to feel like stocks in that industry will keep making you money. Your instinct is to keep pushing it, to keep trying to find new ways to play the same trend that's already made you big profits. I know because I have this instinct too. Investing based on your past success in a sector is wrong; worse than that, it's expensive. When you make money in a stock, don't ever let that make you overconfident. Don't let it influence one bit your judgment about similar stocks in the same industry. Every trade, every investment is different. I don't like to use a gambling analogy, but it will help bring the point home. When you're playing cards and you hit two blackjacks in a row, does that increase or decrease your chances of winning the next hand? You know it does nothing. The cards have no memory, especially when shuffled. The same is true with stocks. We all want to believe in streaks, we want to be streak hitters, and so we look for stocks that fit into our streaks. But even though it feels right, that kind of investing is a surefire way to lose money. When you invest, and you get a stock right, I know it feels to you as though that should have something to do with other stocks. If you make a lot of money in GM, you're going to start thinking that, hey, if GM is so good, maybe Ford can make me money too. It's just how we're programmed, but the programming is wrong. You have to beat your instincts here and not let your past successes poison your ability to judge stocks.

This rule is the Bookham (BKHM) rule. I had to write it after I recommended Bookham, a telecommunications equipment supplier, on February 1, 2006, on the first stop on the Mad Money Back to School Tour, at Harvard Law School. Bookham was the number-two telco equipment supplier by market share, and when I recommended the stock, it was trading at $6.98. I said the stock had upside anywhere from 30 percent to a 100 percent. In April, two and a half months later, the stock peaked a few cents over ten dollars. It would have made a great trade, but I told people to stay in the stock because I had so much confidence in it. By July, Bookham was trading at two dollars and change. I rode it all the way up, and then way back down. The thing that really killed Bookham was Nortel (NT), its biggest customer. When I recommended Bookham, I hated Nortel. It was a terrible company with an even worse stock, and I should have known that it would poison everything it touched. I knew that from my own personal experience losing money in Nortel. But even though Bookham had all that Nortel business, I was still ready and willing to recommend that people buy Bookham. Nortel should have been the red flag that told me to give Bookham a sell, but instead I took the Nortel business in stride and kept telling people to buy.

Why did I make this mistake, and how can you avoid making it yourself? I got Bookham wrong because deep down in my reptilian brain, I believe in streaks and I want to have them. When I got behind Bookham, I'd been having a lot of success speculating on telecommunications equipment suppliers, especially the guys in the fiber-optics end of the business, where Bookham was. Pretty much everybody in the optical components business was raking it in, except of course from Lucent (LU) and Nortel, which were both terrible. I'd recommended both JDS Uniphase (JDSU) and Conexant (CNXT) back in September 2005. Between that September and the day I recommended Bookham, these two stocks could have made you 50, 60, 70, 80, or even 100 percent gains, depending on when you sold. JDS Uniphase and Conexant looked a lot like Bookham. They were all in similar businesses, all three were cheap, under-ten-dollar stocks. All three were speculative. And the first two had made people a lot of money. Because JDSU and CNXT had done so well, I was ready and willing to believe Bookham would do well too. There was a streak—cheap telco suppliers were making people big bucks, and I had been calling the best ones. I was *en fuego*, and the next jewel in my crown would be Bookham.

Just as you should never sell a stock based on panic, a rule from my last book, you should also never buy a stock based on pure triumphalism. I'd gotten JDSU right, I'd gotten CNXT right, and neither of those had a thing to do with whether or not I was going to get Bookham right. I should have evaluated Bookham on its own merits and demerits and not let my desire for a streak cloud my judgment. If I'd seen Bookham more clearly, I would've known that, at the very best, this stock was a short-term trade that would burn you before long because of that Nortel connection. I know this rule seems obvious, but unless you're careful, the obvious things are the ones that will wreck you. I would never have admitted at the time that I liked the stock because I felt as though it fit into my streak. That would be irrational, but that is what was really going on in my head. Investing is emotional and irrational, and you will make bad decisions because of that fact unless you're very careful to keep your emotions in check. If you feel like you've got a streak, like you're totally *en fuego*, that's a sign you need to take a step back, forget about your recent wins, and focus on a stock's fundamentals.

8. Never invest based on borrowed convictions. You and I both know certain things about the market. We have certain beliefs about how stocks trade, about what works in a business and what doesn't. Sometimes those convictions are going to be wrong, and they'll need to be revised or amended. I believe in flexibility above all else, which means you can't rigidly hold to any dogma about stocks. But you also can't throw away your convictions. And you especially can't invest in a stock based on borrowed conviction, meaning someone else's conviction. Maybe it's a CEO's belief in his company, maybe it's the be-

lief of an analyst or a group of analysts. If you don't really believe what an analyst is saying, but the analyst says it with such conviction that you're willing to give him the benefit of the doubt and give the stock a shot, you're making a mistake.

There's a big difference between listening to what a CEO or an analyst has to say and believing them and investing based on borrowed conviction. When you invest based on borrowed conviction, you buy a stock despite the fact that the CEO's belief in his company, or the analyst's belief in the stock, doesn't really make sense to you. When a CEO tells you "This time it'll be different," and he doesn't give you any reason why it will be different, but you believe the guy anyway, that's investing based on borrowed conviction. He's just trying to win you over, like a politician. When a CEO says something plausible and gives good reasons, that's a different story. His conviction becomes your conviction because he convinces you. You should never buy a stock that flies in the face of what you believe about the way the market works.

When it comes to investing, there is no benefit of the doubt. Either you're right or you're wrong. You're going to be wrong a lot. I'm wrong a lot. It doesn't feel good, but it's not the end of the world either, especially if you're right more than you're wrong, or even better, if you're lucky more than you're wrong. But there's one thing that's even worse than getting a stock wrong because you held the wrong conviction, and that's getting a stock wrong because you gave someone the benefit of the doubt who didn't deserve it. You never want to lose money because you borrowed someone else's convictions, especially when you yourself find them suspect. Make your own mistake. Don't beat yourself up extra hard because you stole someone else's.

I'm as guilty of this as the next guy, which is why I wrote the rule for *Mad Money*. On February 28, 2006, I recommended Viropharma (VPHM) at $19.35. Three weeks, just three little weeks later, the stock was trading under $11. I'd bought the hype about the company and said it could easily go to $32. Now, as I write this book in August 2006,

Viropharma has been treading water under $10 for a couple of months. Viropharma was a big mistake, but it's one that you can learn from if you just take a look at what went wrong. I got behind Viropharma for the same reason that a handful of analysts on the Street had liked the stock. It had recently bought a drug called Vancocin from Eli Lilly. Vancocin was the only drug on the market that could treat a certain type of colitis that people tend to contract in hospitals. There's a lot of money to be made selling drugs to hospitals, especially when those drugs treat diseases that the hospitals cause and could potentially be held liable for. Because Vancocin was the only drug on the market that treated this disease, Viropharma had been able to raise prices seriously after it bought the drug from Lilly.

But there was one big problem. Vancocin had gone off patent. Now I know in my bones that off-patent drugs are next to worthless. They cannot make you money because there's nothing proprietary behind them, just a brand name and a drug company. Any generic competitor that feels like it can come along and release the same drug on the market for a lower price. That just ruins your pricing power. You go from having a drug that's a government-protected monopoly to a drug that's the ultimate interchangeable commodity. I knew this about off-patent drugs. I knew it, but Viropharma's management and most of the analysts who covered the stock were certain beyond a shadow of a doubt that it could somehow beat this process. I've never seen a company beat the process. I've never seen a drug company not get hurt when a big drug goes off patent. But Viropharma's management and the analysts who loved them were totally convinced. They never offered a good reason why just the threat of generic competition wouldn't force price cuts, but they were so firm in their belief that I figured they had to know something I didn't.

That was my big mistake, and I don't want you to repeat it. When analysts or executives hold fervently to a belief that you think is wrong, go with your gut, not with the experts. I'm a paranoid guy, so I often think people know some piece of inside information when they make nonsensical claims, but usually they know nothing. Usually when someone says something that makes no sense, especially when he puts a lot of conviction behind it, that person is just wrong. I made this same mistake earlier in Leapfrog (LF), but I didn't take the lesson to heart until I got burned by Viropharma. Leapfrog was a toy company coming out with a pen toy. I didn't really understand the appeal, but there were a few analysts who thought it would be huge, and the same went for the company's management. I let myself be persuaded, not by the content of their arguments, but by their intensity. And I was wrong. Don't ever get sold on a stock because someone else has total conviction in it—use your own conviction. That way, even if you get it wrong, there's nobody else to blame.

9. When you're playing a big rally, make sure your stocks actually fit the bill. Don't be bamboozled by a fuzzy belief that a stock may be levered to a particular sector: know precisely what you own and why you own it. When you think you have a rally in a big-picture sector like health care or technology, you have to be very careful about what you buy. A sectorwide rally, unless it's part of a sector rotation caused by the business cycle, rarely ever happens. But you'll still hear a lot of talk about a "tech rally" or a "health-care rally" or even a "transports rally." When you know there's a rally, but it's being defined nebulously in terms of sectors rather than the industries that compose those sectors, you can't blindly buy anything that you think might fit the bill. You have to be careful and go over your stocks with a fine-tooth comb. What, precisely, is the rally in? Figure out why there is a rally and which companies are actually driving it, then stick with those companies. Don't generalize out to the broader sector, because there probably isn't a broader rally. You have to know what you own and why you own it in the most concrete possible terms, especially when you've got a bullish situation on your hands in which there's a lot of money to be made. You don't want to miss out on the rally, and the way you can make sure you don't is by looking at the actual composition of

the rally, not the hype, and figuring out which stocks will participate in it based on their fundamentals.

This rule came out of one of my biggest mistakes—and also one of my best calls ever. On June 22, 2005, I predicted a major tech rally in the fourth quarter of the year that would probably spill over into the beginning of 2006. I was right generally: there was a big rally within the tech sector over that period of time. But I didn't pay enough attention to the details and probably ended up causing a lot of people to miss the biggest moves of the rally. That happened because on June 22, the same day I called the rally, I wrote MSFT, the symbol for Microsoft, and CSCO, the symbol for Cisco, on my hands. I recommended these stocks not because I thought they were great or even good, but because I had so much conviction in the tech rally that I thought even laggards like Microsoft and Cisco would perform. That was a serious mistake. Tech isn't a single continuous sector. Many tech stocks have nothing in common with the rest of the sector. It's not like the automobile sector where, at the end of the day, everything in it has something to do with cars. Tech has big, important subsectors; the stocks in the tech sector aren't there because their businesses are related. They're there because they sell either products or services that have been branded "technology." It's a confusing way to group stocks, and it even tripped me up.

If you look at the time frame of the tech rally, which I said would occur mostly in the fourth quarter of 2005, but could also stay strong into 2006, Microsoft and Cisco were both disappointing picks. On June 22, when I wrote its ticker symbol on my hand, Microsoft was trading at $25.07 a share. Cisco, on my other hand, had closed at $19.20. Fast-forward to the peak of the rally, which occurred almost exactly where I called it, on February 1, 2006. Microsoft closed that day at $28.04. That's more than an 11-percent increase from where Microsoft closed on June 22. At first glance that looks a whole lot better than a sharp stick in the eye. Cisco was at $18.53 on February 1, roughly a 3.5-percent decline. If you looked at just these numbers, you'd think I was right to recommend Microsoft and that backing Cisco was at worst a minor mistake. But remember, we're dealing with a rally, and you have to compare these two stocks to the stocks that actually participated in the Cramer tech rally. If you saw the writing on my hands you probably bought Microsoft or Cisco instead of a much better stock. Microsoft and Cisco were huge mistakes if you consider the opportunity cost. For example, Broadcom (BRCM) was at $36.43 on June 22 and $68.33 on February 1, an 88-percent gain. Marvell Technology (MRVL) closed at $39.15 on June 22 and went up 73 percent to $67.70 on February 1. Apple (AAPL) went from $38.55 to $75.42, a 96-percent increase. Even if you look at a less impressive performer like Qualcomm (QCOM), which went from $34.92 on June 22 to $47.93 on February 1, you're still dealing with a 37-percent gain. In light of these numbers, Microsoft and Cisco were both mistakes of the highest order, because owning them prevented you from making big money in other tech names.

What did I do wrong, and how can you stop yourself from making the same mistake? I didn't make sure the stocks I was recommending were actually levered to the rally when I told you to buy Cisco and Microsoft. I painted with too broad a brush. The rally in "tech" that I'd called was actually a rally in gadgets and the companies that make gadget components. It was an iPod, cell phone, PlayStation Portable, Palm Pilot, BlackBerry rally, a gadget rally. And I knew that when I declared the rally on June 22 because I said the rally would be driven by tech product cycles. These gadget companies all have their own product cycles, cycles that would be moving up toward their peak in the fourth quarter of 2005 and the first quarter of 2006. The gadget makers were coming out with new devices, and they were set to move a lot of merchandise. I knew this was a gadget-driven rally, but I still wrote MSFT and CSCO on my hands for emphasis, because I believed that strength in one part of tech would lead to strength in all parts of tech. It turns out that a rising tide does not lift all ships.

If I had known about this rule when I announced the arrival of the Cramer tech rally, I would have made sure to figure out the precise cause of the rally and then looked over all the stocks I was talking about to be certain that they were levered to the thing causing the rally: product cycles in high-tech gadgets. Cisco, which makes networking gear, had no exposure to the actual cause of the rally. Microsoft had some exposure to the rally, because its operating systems are in some phones and handheld devices, but it was barely a participant. I should not have written either of these names on my hands, because even though they're generally seen as representing "tech," they weren't levered to gadget product cycles and thus weren't part of the rally. Especially when there's a lot of money to be made, but even when there isn't, you need to know what you own and why you own it. The Street can be dumb, but it's not so dumb that it will mark up stocks that appear to be associated with a rally but actually aren't. As long as you pay careful attention to the reasons why your stock should go higher, and you make sure those reasons make sense, you won't miss out on another opportunity like the Cramer tech rally by buying the wrong stocks.

10. Don't try to smash iconic truths; try to make money. The conventional wisdom is conventional for a reason. Big institutional investors generally all behave pretty much the same way. Sometimes they look irrational or even stupid for buying and selling certain stocks at certain times. I am often tempted to try to beat the institutions by figuring out the way they operate, looking for moves that seem stupid and using them either as opportunities to buy a stock they've knocked down for a bad reason or to sell a stock they've marked up for a similarly bad reason. When the hedge funds and the mutual funds do the same exact thing, year after year, and it doesn't look like it makes them any money, don't jump to the conclusion that they're being hidebound idiots. Sometimes they're just being careful, and it pays to be careful. It doesn't necessarily pay to demolish the conventional

wisdom; being an iconoclast is only rarely profitable. So don't be arrogant when you see trading patterns that don't make any sense to you. Be cautious, figure out why the funds play the game the way they do, and if they're motivated by fear, respect that fear. Panic loses people money, but a healthy fear of unnecessary risk will only save you money.

I had to impose this rule on myself after my horrible experience recommending Montpelier Re Holdings (MRH). Montpelier was a reinsurance company—that's an insurance company that insures regular insurance companies. When I recommended this stock on August 26, 2005, at $33.72 a share, I was being both arrogant and incautious. I thought I'd spotted a great way to trade insurance companies. Every year during hurricane season the insurance companies would all get marked down. Lots of the hedge funds and mutual funds would sell these stocks in the fear that they would end up having to pay for a lot of hurricane damage. For the last few years the insurance companies would get sold down during this period in August and September, and then right after hurricane season, they would raise their premiums and bounce back even higher. The hurricanes wouldn't do serious damage to the insurance companies because, as I told people who were watching, the insurance companies expected and budgeted for hurricanes. The selling by the big funds ahead of and during hurricane season was sheer panic—or at least that's what I said—and panic gives you a chance to make money. I said that all the talk of hurricanes and the worry about them was pure hype. If you wanted to make money, you had to see through the hype. My pitch was that hurricane season would cause the big institutions to act irrationally and sell off and mark down great insurance companies like Montpelier and you'd have a chance to buy them on the cheap before they bounced back up.

Let me give you a timeline of Montpelier's implosion after I recommended that people buy it on any weakness. On August 29, three days after I got behind Montpelier, Hurricane Katrina hit land in

Louisiana and the levees in New Orleans started to breach. That day Montpelier closed at $34.03. A week later, on September 6, the stock was at $32.29. That looked like the kind of markdown I talked about when I told people to buy the stock. Maybe it was a buying opportunity? Maybe not. A week after that, when the monetary cost of Katrina for Montpelier, which had foolishly written most of the policies in the Southeast, essentially putting all of its eggs in one vulnerable, Gulf-Coast basket, had started to become apparent, the stock closed at $25.99. If you were still listening to my original advice at this point, you might have seen Montpelier at $26 as the result of pure panic selling, making it a great buying opportunity. That would have been wrong. Hurricane Rita made landfall in Texas and Louisiana on September 24, and on the September 26, the first trading day after Rita hit, Montpelier closed at $26.19. By October 3, a week after that, it was down to $24.87. Once all the financial damage from Katrina and Rita started to be calculated, and Montpelier started having to pay out a lot of money, the stock really got hammered. By November 7, the stock had come down to $18.75. As I write this book, Montpelier has traded roughly between $15 and $20 ever since. The stock got crushed and stayed crushed.

It wasn't just two bad hurricanes that hurt Montpelier. Because it had foolishly concentrated a lot of its business along the Gulf Coast, because it hadn't stopped insuring at-risk customers, as Allstate intelligently decided to do, Montpelier ended up having to pay out a lot more money than it actually had on hand. In order to pay off the policies it had written, Montpelier had to do a secondary public offering. It had to create new shares of stock, effectively giving each existing share less of a stake in the company, and then sell those shares to raise money. Montpelier had to do this at the worst possible time, after its stock had already been smacked around by the two hurricanes. That meant it had to sell many more shares because it was getting less money for each share. Naturally, that helped keep Montpelier's stock price down.

Unfortunately, I can't blame Montpelier on chance or on the weather. I recommended the stock not in spite of the hurricanes, but because of them. I looked at this habit that the big institutional investors had of selling off insurance companies during hurricane season, and I didn't give it any respect. I tried to game it without understanding it. If I'd had this rule at the time, I wouldn't have recommended Montpelier. I would have spent more time thinking about why these funds were selling insurance stocks, and I would have realized that they sold them not in panic, but because of a healthy, intelligent sense of fear. Montpelier dropped more than 40 percent in less than three months after I recommended it. These funds were right to be afraid. If I'd been afraid with them, I could have avoided giving a buy to a stock that was only going straight down. Montpelier just was not worth the risk. Even if the two hurricanes had been mild, I doubt the stock would have been up more than 10 percent in the next six months, and it certainly wouldn't have been up 40 percent in the first two and a half months. Even if a hurricane that bad for insurance companies hits only once every ten years, the risk-reward still favors selling the insurance stocks, just in case.

You don't have to repeat the mistake I made in Montpelier. Don't write off the habits of your fellow investors, especially the ones that look stupid and incomprehensible. Usually people have decent reasons for buying and selling stocks, and you should understand those reasons thoroughly before you try to game the supposed "stupidity" of your fellow investors.

Those are my ten new rules, gleaned from ten of my most embarrasing and educational mistakes on *Mad Money*. Some of these rules help introduce my new approach to the market, an approach that stresses understanding how hedge funds and mutual funds operate, because they control so much of the money in the market and think so alike that they essentially set stock prices. Other rules are just new lessons that I've learned from making mistakes and constantly reevaluating my judgments and actions on the show in light of those mistakes. These new rules are every bit as important as my last set of rules in *Real Money,* and they're also more up-to-date. It's important that you respect them, because I created them to stop you, and stop myself, from making the mistakes I've already made on the show. It's better for you to learn from my mistakes, which cost you nothing, than it is for you to learn from your own mistakes, because who knows how much money you'll have to lose before you come up with these insights. Stick with my rules, add the new ones to the old ones, obey the disciplines laid out in the first chapters of this book about home-work, buying, and selling, and you'll have an edge on just about every other individual and institutional investor out there.

And hey, if you see me make a mistake on the show, if you think I've pulled another Dick's Sporting Goods or Energy Partners, I want you to call me on it. Seriously, call me at 1-800-743-CNBC. I'll take your call, especially if it's critical of my stock picks. You need me to help you invest like a pro, but I need you to help keep me honest. You hold my feet to the fire. Your participation in the show isn't just good for you, it's good for me and good for everyone else who watches.

9

TEN LESSONS
FROM SUCCESS

Some Buy and
Sell Rules

Just as I've spent countless hours trying to learn from my worst calls on the show, I spend nearly as much time trying to draw lessons from my best calls. It's easier to learn from your mistakes than it is to learn from your successes. When you make money on a stock, sometimes you just got lucky and there's nothing more to it than that. When you make a bad call, you're never allowed to write it off to bad luck—you always have to keep digging until you figure out what you could have done better. There also isn't as much incentive to learn from your best calls. Whenever you get a stock right, there's a big temptation just to sit back and assume you have some special talent. I don't believe that. There are no talented and untalented investors. There are just people who have the right disciplines and people who have the wrong ones—or worse, people who have no disciplines at all. That's why you often can learn a lot from your good calls; you can try to figure out what those good disciplines are or what they should be. When

I make a good call on *Mad Money*, I don't just rest on my laurels—I try to learn.

I've developed ten more rules from carefully examining the stocks I got right. I'm not treating stocks that I recommended as "investments" any differently from my "trades." At this point, the market has become complicated enough that the only real difference between a trade and an investment is that with a trade, you know your exit strategy ahead of time, and with an investment, you have to figure it out as you go along. But now there are few stocks that are worth owning—for even eighteen months. Most things go up, and then they'll get hit with something—an earnings shortfall, a sector rotation, bad press—you name it. As the global economy has become more integrated, owning stocks has become more complicated and more difficult. There are more things you, as a shareholder, need to keep track of if you don't want to get burned. Five years ago resin costs—that's just what a company pays for plastic—were a stable and unimportant part of investing. Now you need to pay attention to resin costs, because they've gotten higher and become more volatile. That's just one example out of many.

That's why I'm not drawing any distinction between my best "trades" on the show and my best "investments." I'm just looking at my best calls. How did I get these stocks right? Six of my rules come out of stocks I told you to buy that went up; the other four are products of my best sell calls. It's just as important to know when to sell as it is to know what to buy. Knowing when to bail out and give up on a stock entirely is much harder and requires more discipline than knowing what to buy. I say this because that is what I've learned from systematically analyzing my best calls on the show over the past year. My very best calls have been the ones that prevented you from losing money; that's why it's important to learn the rules behind what made them good calls.

We'll start with the six rules I've learned from the show that make for a good buy, and then I'll give you the four rules that underlie a great sell. Just like the rules that I created by looking at my worst calls, the rules behind my best calls aren't about the individual investor trying to make money in the market; they're about the individual investor trying to make money in a market that's almost entirely dominated by a small number of large institutional buyers and sellers, the hedge funds and mutual funds. The money managers at these funds generally think and behave alike, as I've already said. By analyzing their behavior, which very quickly becomes the behavior of the "market," you can systematically approach investing in a way that works.

1. Follow the Street's lead: most of the time it works. When you trade based on momentum, buying a stock that's gone up in the expectation that the momentum will take it higher, or when you buy a stock that belongs to a group that's been favored or "anointed" by the big institutional investors, you're trying to make money by following the Street's lead. Unless you believe that these hedge funds and mutual funds are dead wrong about a stock, you can get rich just by looking at their past behavior and anticipating what they'll do in the future. If the big funds have started buying bank stocks hand over fist, it's not a bad bet that the banks will go higher. How can you tell that the big funds are buying? When a stock goes up significantly and there hasn't been a takeover bid, you can be pretty sure it's going up because big institutions are buying it. The same is true when a stock goes down significantly. Of course, you can't rely on the Street to make your decisions for you, and you're never allowed to buy a stock just because it's going up. However, once you've done all the necessary homework, and if you believe that a stock has good fundamentals and a good story, then looking at how the Street approaches it can be a useful way to help decide whether or not you should buy it. This may be more true with stocks than it is with sectors. If you have trouble spotting the stocks I'm talking about, a casual glance at the new-high list for the New York Stock Exchange or the NASDAQ

speaks loudly about what's working. Those stocks don't get on the new-high list for nothing.

I've already told you not to fight the business cycle because then you'll be fighting the funds, and when you do that you lose. That's similar to this rule, but this rule is broader. You may know that the oil and gas sector is surging, but you'll make even more money if you also know that ConocoPhillips (COP) is the best performing of the major integrated oil companies. That means it's the integrated oil that's been "anointed" by the Street. It's the one that the funds think of first when they decide they want more oil exposure, and thus it's the one they buy more of. If you pay attention to the stocks the big institutional investors have anointed, you can anticipate the moves of those big buyers and make yourself a lot money.

The best example on *Mad Money* of an investment that came out of going with the flow on Wall Street was Allegheny Technologies (ATI). I made this company my stock of the year for 2006 on February 3 when the stock was at $36.05. A month later, on March 3, my stock of the year closed at $50.98, up 41 percent from where I picked it. Four months later, the stock was up 72 percent, at $62.02. On May 3, five months later, it closed at $71.47, up 98 percent. Between May 3 and the peak on May 11, the stock went as high as $84.53. Even after the peak, as I write this in August, it has never gone below $55, and it mostly hovered around $60. I was telling people to clear out of this stock shortly before the peak, to take at least a little, but preferably a lot, off the table. After you catch a double in a stock, discipline tells you to take those gains to the bank. Even if you didn't listen to me when I said sell, you still made a lot of money in this stock. How did I help you do it?

I did it by following the lead of the big money managers. Sure, Allegheny had great fundamentals. It is a company that manufactures titanium and stainless steel, and the market for both of those products, especially titanium, was incredibly strong at the time. The titanium market was being strengthened by a strong aerospace cycle.

Because titanium is strong but much lighter than steel, it makes for more fuel-efficient airplanes. These were all great fundamental reasons to buy the stock. But they're not what brought it to my attention, and they're not why it worked so well.

The big reasons I talked about Allegheny on the show, the reason I made it my stock of the year, was that Titanium Metals (TIE) had been the best-performing stock of 2005. As you can imagine, Titanium Metals makes titanium. From this I knew that the big funds wanted titanium exposure. I knew that they felt good about buying titanium stocks because they'd made a lot of money in Titanium Metals. I assumed they would try to expand their titanium exposure, and they'd do it by swapping out of Titanium Metals, where the easy money had already been made, and swapping into Allegheny Tech, a company that wasn't pure titanium, but that was expanding its titanium business. I looked at what the Street had liked in 2005, and then I picked out a stock that looked similar to it for 2006. Sure enough, the big institutions did what they always do: they look at what's been working for them and they buy more of it. Allegheny Technologies was a great pick because it both followed and anticipated the behavior of the big institutional players. They're the ones who drove the stock higher. Yes, the stock had great fundamentals and the money managers absolutely paid attention to them, but there were stocks with better fundamentals that didn't double over a five-month period. Allegheny worked both because it had great fundamentals and because the Street was eyeing the stock hungrily. If you watch what's been working and what hasn't, you can come up with great investment ideas. The big money managers who set prices are creatures of habit: if a stock or a type of stock has been earning profits, they'll throw even more capital into similar stocks. When you anticipate this behavior, you can make serious money.

2. How to be a contrarian and still make money. I just told you to go with the flow, but there are times where you make a lot of money by

going against the conventional wisdom and buying a stock that's totally out of favor. That said, you have to know what you're doing. Not
every hated stock becomes a winner. Most of them keep being hated
and keep going down. If you're going to buy a stock that you think the
big institutions are wrong about, you have to do more than just your
regular homework. You still must understand the fundamentals of
the company; you need to know how the market treats the sector; you
have to know that the stock you're buying is good. But you must add
one more thing if it's a stock that's seemingly out of favor: you must
understand why the big institutional money managers and/or the
analysts will change their minds about the stock. If they don't change
their minds then no matter how good the company is, no matter how
great the fundamentals, you know that stock is not going higher.

The way to make good, contrarian calls is by understanding what
will make a stock move from the out-of-favor column into the in-
favor column. You need to know how the money managers think, and
for that, you should watch me think out loud on *Mad Money*. There
are some easy ways to tell what the institutional investors are thinking
about a stock. If the earnings estimates for a stock are all low, and you
think that the company is going to blow those earnings away, then
you have a good thesis. If the fund managers don't like the stock because they think the earnings will be bad, then they will like it more
when the earnings turn out to be better. Usually it's a little bit more
complicated than that, but you can see how the basic logic operates.
If you can't explain why a hated stock will suddenly become loved by
the big institutions, you can't buy it. Stocks that are hated don't go up
a lot. First they must become liked but if not loved, because after all,
stocks are just pieces of paper.

Two of my best contrarian calls were Amylin Pharmaceuticals
(AMLN) and Google (GOOG) at the very beginning of the show.
People might not think of Google as an out-of-favor stock at this
point, but from its IPO in August 2004 until about a year later, this

stock was unloved. It was being valued at a huge discount to competitors like Yahoo! Investors were wary of the stock, and even some of the analysts who were giving Google high earnings estimates were telling their clients to stay away. Amylin is a small drug company that specializes in treatments for diabetes. When I got behind it in June 2005, it was one of the most heavily shorted, most despised stocks out there. When I recommended both of these companies, I stressed not just the good fundamental story, but also what would cause the institutional investors to stop hating them and start buying them.

Even though it already had a drug on the market, Amylin was basically a one-drug story for me when I recommended it on June 13, 2005, at $17.63 a share. That drug was Byetta, and it hit the market the day I told people to buy the stock. Most of the analysts covering the company, and most of the Street, which was either ignoring or shorting the company, thought Byetta would be a nothing drug. It treated type 2 diabetes, and even though the clinical trials had shown it was very effective, the Street didn't think it would sell because it had to be injected. I disagreed. The stock broke through $30 on August 26, $40 on December 20, and touched $50 on July 5, 2006. This stock did not go up because I was right about Byetta sales and the Street was wrong. The stock went up because the Street changed its mind. It came around to Cramer's view. When I recommended the stock, I knew that the big institutions would start to like it if Byetta sales exceeded the low expectations that the Street had set for them, or if new applications or new versions of the drug were introduced. Why would this change their minds? The Street hated Amylin because they thought its drug wouldn't sell; they thought it was hype. I know this because Amylin was practically a one-drug stock: if you liked Byetta, you liked Amylin, and if you hated Byetta, you hated Amylin. I'd done my homework and thought the drug would work—the Street's objections were silly. Most diabetics already inject insulin, so having to inject Byetta, a more effective drug than others on the market, didn't seem to me like much of a drawback. I was right, but again, what mattered was that the Street was willing to repudiate its old position and agree with mine.

The story behind Google was similar. Everyone knew that Google had tremendous growth and earnings power, but people were hesitant to buy it, and most of the analysts were telling people to sell it all the way up. The big institutions were staying away from Google, which was priced at $178.61 on the first day *Mad Money* aired, March 15, 2005, but which I'd been recommending from the IPO in August 2004 at $100. The big institutions that run the market disliked Google for irrational reasons, but irrationally can rule the market. Most of the money managers on the Street had gotten incredibly burned by big internet IPOs in the late 1990s and 2000. They still felt like anything that made its money from a Web site had to be all hype. When it came to Google they were wrong, because Google was making boatloads of money, and it had steroidal growth. But how did I know they would change their minds? I saw what all the high-growth mutual funds were paying for Yahoo!, Google's closest competitor. It was a whole lot more than what they were paying for Google, based on P/E or PEG. They weren't paying as much for Google because it was a newly public company and they didn't have faith it could deliver the earnings or the growth the Street was predicting. I knew that once Google had reported enough good quarters, the big growth mutual funds and the negative analysts would forget about the dot-com stigma attached to Google and just buy the stock. But they needed reassurance before they bought; they needed good quarter after good quarter to get rid of their lack of conviction. Once these guys started to change their minds, the stock couldn't stop going higher.

How is this any different from another company reporting lots of good quarters and going up? The point here is that Google was undervalued because the big institutions were approaching it irrationally. The hedge funds and the mutual funds are usually pretty rational when they approach stocks, at least where earnings are concerned. If a company reports a bunch of good quarters, its stock might not do anything. It might even go down. But when a stock is out of favor because the institutions don't have any faith it will hit the estimates—not for any real reason, but because they've gotten burned by similar stocks in the past—when that stock reports good quarters and good earnings, that really matters. Good earnings make a difference when they change minds. If you look for situations where the big institutions all essentially agree, are all negative, and you think they're wrong, you have to be able to point to some catalyst that will cause the institutions to change their minds. Otherwise you won't make much money. Always remember that the big institutions out there *have* to own stocks. That forces them to value stocks. When the portfolio managers took a hard look at GOOG, they recognized that it was going to have to get the highest multiple on its earnings because it was growing faster than every other large-cap company. Once they attached the highest multiple and solved for P, or price, that got them to $400, which is where I pegged the stock even when it was in the $200s.

3. The street is never bullish enough on good stocks, and it's never bearish enough on bad stocks. When the analysts who cover stocks in a given sector are bullish, and you agree with them, then you should get behind that sector and buy more of your favorite stock in it. If the Street is bearish about a sector and you agree, you should stay out of the whole thing. In general, the analysts who cover stocks will never be bullish enough when they're positive, and they'll never be bearish enough when they're negative. That means you have an opportunity. If the analysts like a stock that you like, you should like it more than the analysts. You should think it's going higher than the analysts think it's going. By the same token, if you see that all the analysts are bearish on a sector, but still recommending some stocks in it, don't buy those stocks.

The analysts never got behind oil and natural gas in 2004 and 2005 the way that they should have. They may have been mildly bullish, but they missed one of the greatest bull markets in recent history by not being bullish enough. The analysts thought the increase in oil prices was caused by high demand, but they were wrong. It was a combination of short supply and high demand. I was behind oil and natural gas, pretty much anything in the oil patch, from the very beginning of the show, and I rode that sector all the way up because I understood that even though the Street was bullish, it should have been a lot more bullish. The Street had to get behind these stocks in the end because they set a price for the commodity, and when the price was breached and breached and breached again, they were dragged kicking and screaming into recommending the stocks because both their estimates and their price targets were too low. But remember, they did nothing but follow the stocks up; they never led them. That's your way to win as an individual investor anticipating the estimate bumps upward.

Then when you look at bad stocks like Boston Scientific (BSX), Amazon.com (AMZN), eBay (EBAY), or Lucent (LU), stocks that I went negative on before their precipitous declines, you'll also see that the analysts were never bearish enough. Sure, they didn't like these stocks, but they never hated them with a passion, which is what they deserved. When real estate and housing went into free fall, the analysts were still recommending one or two home builders, even though the sector was terrible. I was telling people to stay the heck away from all the home builders.

The same thing happened with Vonage (VG)—the dog, the worst IPO of the first half of 2006—and with all the radio stocks. I said Vonage was terrible before it came public, and all it did was go straight down after the initial public offering. The analysts would have been more negative, but they worked for the investment banks that were making a lot of money taking the company public. I know that Eliot Spitzer is supposed to have cleaned up Wall Street, but I don't think there's an impenetrable wall at the investment banks between the analysts and everyone else. The analysts, if they are smart and want big raises, will recommend the stocks that do business with the banks they work for. They had to get behind VG. They helped price it at $17, so they had to like it at $15, $12, $10, and so on.

As for radio, the Street was negative here, but it wasn't as negative as it should have been. I said radio was dead. I said print media was dead too, and in both cases I was right, but the analysts continued to recommend newspaper stocks and radio stocks. I said radio was dead even though I have a radio show that obviously needs the radio companies to back it, but I don't care about those guys; I'm looking out for your interests. The analysts couldn't agree: they had to recommend some radio stock or what was the point of covering the industry in the first place? If you can read the analysts as I do on the show, then you can make a lot of money. When the analysts are mildly bullish, you should be extremely bullish, as long as you think they're right. When they're mildly bearish, you should sell everything in the sector they are bearish about. The reason the analysts are never bullish or bearish enough just has to do with the way analysts are trained and told to do their jobs. Most analysts on the Street are assigned to cover a single, specific sector. They'll cover a number of stocks in that sector. Since they're specialists in the sector, it's not hard for them to get the broader, general picture right. But because of the way investment banks work, analysts aren't allowed to have buy ratings on all the stocks they cover. They have to have some sells and some holds no matter what. That means if oil is totally on fire, and all the oil stocks are going much higher, an oil analyst still has to tell you to sell a couple of those stocks, and he still has to put a tepid hold on a couple of others. This makes him look a lot more bearish than he actually is. The reverse is also true. If the telecommunications equipment makers are all about to get cut in half because telco spending is about to be frozen, a telco equipment analyst still has to have a couple of buys and a couple of holds, even if he believes the whole sector is a sell.

Luckily, we don't have to play by those rules. You can rule out whole sectors—that's what I do on *Mad Money*. And when you find a good sector, you can run with it, even if the analysts are already bullish, because you know that they're not bullish enough. Sometimes people feel like they're chasing a sector, like they've missed the boat, if all the analysts are already positive. There are times when that's true, when you've hit a top, but most of the time, when the analysts are bullish, you'll win by being even more bullish.

4. Don't be a snob. Some of the best trends are completely hidden from Wall Street. Remember, analysts and especially money managers belong to a tiny group of incredibly rich people, mostly clustered around Manhattan. They're far from omniscient. Lots of things pass completely under their radar because they live in a bubble. This fact has created many opportunities for me and may make you a lot of money. Because all the people who run money tend to be rich, or at the very least tend to spend money as if they were rich, they often miss trends in mid-grade or low-end products, companies, and stocks. They don't shop at these places. They're not aware of what's going on because they all buy their clothes at Saks and eat dinner at The Palm. By the same token, retailers, banks, and restaurants without a presence in the New York metro area also often pass under the radar of money managers. If these companies are good, they'll eventually come to the attention of the Street, but for a brief period you can buy them while they're unnoticed.

JCPenney (JCP) is a classic example of a stock that made you money from Wall Street snobbery. I recommended JCPenney on December 20, 2005, when the stock traded at $54.51. In March 2006 the stock broke through $60, and it hasn't looked back since. If you'd sold at any point while the stock was over $65, where it was for most of June, then you would have had a better than 20 percent return. What happened with JCPenney was simple. The company had been a wreck, but then it went through a really significant turnaround. The problem was that nobody on Wall Street noticed the changes at JCPenney.

They didn't notice because they never shop there. Maybe they bought venetian blinds there when they went to college, but that's about the extent of their contact with the company. I'm serious: it's just that simple. The guys on Wall Street are all going to Neiman Marcus or Saks or Nordstrom; they wouldn't be caught dead in a JCPenney. Even the analysts who cover the stock don't want to actually go to any JCPenney stores. It's too downscale for them, even though Penney is a middle-of-the-road department store. Most of the big institutions missed out on a large part of JCPenney's move from $54 to $65, but I didn't, because I'm not a snob. I go to JCPenney, and even if I never shopped there, I still know better than to write the stock off just because it's not on my own personal radar.

The same exact thing happened with Darden Restaurants (DRI) and GameStop (GME). I liked both of these stocks from before *Mad Money* began, and they both had pretty continuous runs up ever since the show started. Darden is the company that owns the Olive Garden and Red Lobster. Nobody on the Street, not even the analysts who cover Darden, will go to either of these places. I consistently got behind Darden whenever anyone called in about the stock. I pleaded with people not to be snobs and to actually go to the Olive Garden, where the food is pretty good and there's always a long wait for a table. The stock moved up from $27.12 to more than $40 between March 15, 2005, and January 2006. I got help: my kids hate fancy food, and I am not going to waste good money going to upscale restaurants with them. The Street missed this move, most of the big institutional buyers missed this move, but you didn't miss this move if you watched *Mad Money* and you didn't act like a snob when you picked stocks.

The situation with GameStop was slightly different, but it followed the same pattern. GameStop sells video games, and because most analysts and money managers don't play video games, they ignored the stock. I liked the stock, even owned it for my charitable trust, from before the show started. On the first day of the show, March 15,

2005, the stock closed at $21.19. By June 1, the stock hit $30, and by January 31, 2006, it had broken through $40. My daughters play video games, and some of my coworkers do too, so I wasn't oblivious to the great things that were happening at GameStop. Because video games were on my radar, but not Wall Street's, I had an opportunity to buy the stock cheap, before the Street figured out what was going on.

If you can recognize the limitations of the analysts and the big institutional money managers, you can learn to spot opportunities. These guys are snobs, and they're very limited in where they go and what they do for fun. Any stock with great fundamentals that's outside the Wall Street bubble is a stock that can make you a lot of money.

5. Pay attention to politics, because the Street is too focused on money. There are a lot of companies that make their money feeding off the U.S. government. There are even more companies that could potentially strike it rich because Congress decides to send a little bit of pork their way. The analysts on Wall Street, and most of the money managers, tend not to focus on any of this stuff. They're too focused on how companies make their money and not focused enough on what could happen in Washington to increase profits. I think differently. I believe we have a government of, by, and for the corporations that will not rest until it finds more ways to subsidize big business. Maybe you don't like that politically, but I don't care about politics. I care about making you rich, and that means paying attention to government spending. This is another area in which you can get ahead of the analysts and ahead of all the big institutional investors. Getting in ahead of the hedge funds and the mutual funds means making boatloads of money, because when these guys catch a whiff of something they like, they send the stocks up into the stratosphere.

I learned this by playing around with ethanol stocks. I recommended Archer Daniels Midland (ADM), the largest processor of ethanol in the country, on August 22, 2005, when the stock was at

$21.90. This was well before ethanol became a big fad in the press and on Wall Street. I had realized that with high oil prices, ethanol—a fuel long subsidized by the government because the Iowa corn growers, who all vote first in presidential primaries, have a lot of political clout—would become a lot more economically viable and a lot more politically favored. The Street wasn't watching any of this. None of the big institutions figured out how important ethanol would be until much later, really the beginning of 2006, when every political figure in America started talking about the importance of using ethanol as fuel. Because I paid attention to politics, I knew they were going to pump ethanol even before it happened. Politicians all want to be president, so they all pander to the same constituencies in Iowa and New Hampshire, the early primary states. Archer Daniels hit $30 on January 31, 2006, and it hit $40 on May 2. The stock peaked above $46. If you'd bought when I told you to and sold before the peak on May 11, there was a very real chance that you could have caught a double.

Another example of how the Street's ignorance of all things political can make you rich was my recommendation of Anglo American (AAUK) on September 29, 2005, at $30.05. Anglo American is a mining company that primarily produces gold, platinum, and diamonds. The analysts on the Street thought this company would make its money by selling gold for jewelry. They weren't paying attention to politics. People in China, India, and even Iran were buying twenty-four-karat gold, which is too soft for jewelry, because they didn't trust their governments not to run large amounts of inflation. When people are afraid of inflation, they buy gold because it holds its value much better than, say, the rupee, India's currency. But none of the analysts saw this coming. I did, and the stock ramped up to $39 by January 27, 2006, and then after a two-for-one split, it hit $22 on April 19, which if you adjust for the split means it hit $44. That's almost a 50-percent gain all because the Street didn't pay any attention to the value of gold as a hedge against third-world inflation.

We made that money by focusing on the political aspects of investing, aspects that Wall Street tends to ignore because it's too caught up in the money and not caught up enough in the forces that create more money.

6. There's a rhythm to investing in small-cap stocks with momentum and not much analyst coverage. If you know the rhythm, you'll make money and avoid getting burned. In my last book I talked about small-cap stocks with little analyst coverage that become the flavor of the year and take off. They go higher and higher as more and more funds see that they're performing and decide they want to get in on the action. The stocks also start to attract more and more attention from analysts, who tell people to buy the stock because it has been going up and they don't want to fight the momentum. There's a simple and easy way to speculate on these stocks, but in *Real Money* I didn't have an example, so I didn't make it into a rule. On *Mad Money* I found an example, and it's one that I played perfectly. With these stocks, you want to ride them all the way up, obviously taking some off the table as per my earlier instructions, but once enough analysts are telling people to buy the stock, once it starts trading at more than twice its growth rate and the stock has become priced for perfection, that's when you bail.

I have an example to show you exactly how this works. When I started *Mad Money* on March 15, 2005, not a single analyst covered Hansen Natural (HANS), a company that makes natural sodas. It had, however, already been one of the best-performing stocks of 2004 and 2005. I was bullish on this stock from the day I started the show, when it cost $58.44 a share. By July 18, 2005, the stock had acquired one analyst who gave it a buy, and it had broken through $100. At that point, you should have taken a little off the table, but I also knew that this ride was far from finished. These small stocks with little coverage all have a rhythm, and if you follow that rhythm, you can make a lot of money and avoid getting burned. After a two-for-one split and another analyst initiating coverage and giving the stock a buy, Hansen was back up to $80 by December 2, 2005, which is $160 if you adjust for the split. If a stock has acquired two analysts as it runs up, you're still in the safe zone; it still has room to go higher. By May 8, 2006, Hansen had crossed $150—that's $300 if you adjust for the split—and acquired another analyst. Discipline says you have to take some off the table, but with three analysts on it, the stock still had legs. On July 5, Hansen broke through $200 a share, which means $400 adjusted for the split, and I'd started telling people to cash out.

After a four-for-one split, the stock went below $30 a share on August 7, which means $120 before the four-for-one and $240 before the split before that. That's a big decline, and I got you out before the decline. I got you out because I knew two simple things about small-cap momentum stocks with little analyst coverage. One, when one of these stocks has four analysts on it, has become too well publicized and too widely praised. Everyone who's going to recommend it already has, and everybody who's going to buy the stock has already bought it. Four analysts is the upper limit. Three analysts can be pushing it, but that depends on the second component. Once the stock is trading at more than twice its growth rate—that means it has a PEG greater than 2—you want to get out. This usually won't happen until there are at least three analysts on the stock. So if you want to play this game, here are the rules. You can buy the stock as long as there are fewer than four analysts on it and as long as it is trading at less than twice its growth rate. More than that and the stock has become priced for perfection and ready for a fall, which is exactly what happened to Hansen. As long as you keep these rules in mind, you'll be able to make a lot of money investing in small-cap stocks with momentum and not much analyst coverage.

Those are the rules that I've created after carefully examining some of my best buy recommendations on the show. I have four more rules that come out of my best sell calls. It's more important to avoid losing money than it is to make money. If you're doing the homework and being careful, then your money should practically make itself.

How can you make the right sell calls?

7. Use tips as a contraindicator. Whenever you start getting "tips" about a stock, that's a good time for you to stop buying, start doing some homework, and probably sell the thing. In my last book I told you that tips are for waiters. If a tip is good, it must be inside information, and therefore it's illegal. Every other kind of tip is based on publicly available information that most investors in a stock are already familiar with. If it's old news, it can't make you money. As I put together *Mad Money* every day I am deluged with stock tips. I've come to realize that they actually can be useful. Tips are a great reason to sell a stock. Tips indicate that there are a lot of investors in a stock for the wrong reasons. When people own a stock but they don't understand it, they can be shaken out at even the slightest sign of bad news. They're bad fellow shareholders because they haven't done the homework and they really don't have a clue what they're doing. A stock that is generating lots of tips is full of these in-it-for-the-wrong-reasons, cut-and-run investors. I'm not saying you should just clear out and sell off your whole position in a stock when you get a tip, but you should absolutely go back, redo all the preliminary homework, and make sure that stock isn't headed for a fall.

On the show, I realized that stock tips could be great reasons to sell a stock when I was looking at Amylin Pharmaceuticals (AMLN) in July 2006. Amylin, as you already know, was a stock I'd caught very low and ridden all the way up to the top. But on July 20, I got an e-mail from a viewer with a tip about Amylin. The e-mail said that the viewer, who was both a doctor and a diabetic, knew a well-kept secret about Amylin's drug Byetta: it causes weight loss. He said that this secret was quietly becoming known to many doctors and that it would eventually cause the stock to go a lot higher. When I read this,

I was ready to hit the sell button, or even the triple-sell button. The fact that Byetta causes weight loss was well publicized and had been known even before the drug's release on the market. There was no secret. What did I learn from this e-mail? I learned that there must be a lot of investors who were in Amylin for the wrong reasons and that these investors would dump the stock at the first big decline, because they're bozos who can't take the pain. Before I came out on the show and told people to sell the stock, I went back and did a little homework. Amylin was having supply problems with Byetta; they couldn't make enough of the cartridges to meet demand. That's a high-quality problem, but it's still a problem. To me, that meant that the next time Amylin reported earnings, it was going to disappoint and the stock would get crushed. I came out on *Mad Money* and told everyone this, that the stock was much hyped, priced for perfection, and ready to go down. On July 20, when I said all of that, Amilyn was priced at $49.91. Three weeks later, by August 11, the stock was down to $41.23, a 17 percent decline. Tips aren't just for waiters, they're great contraindicators that tell good investors to sell.

8. Hype plus massive short interest equals sell. Whenever you see a stock that's heavily hyped, and also heavily shorted, you should sell. Hype is a combination of analyst recommendations, celebrity endorsements, and much-praised facts about a company that don't necessarily have anything to do with making money. Back in the late 1990s and in 2000, Internet stocks traded off of hype—people bought them based on the number of page clicks or unique new visitors, not on earnings or revenues. Eventually all these stocks crashed and burned; that's how hype works as a great contrary indicator. You can find the short interest in a stock just by going to Yahoo! Finance, typing in the stock symbol, then clicking the Key Statistics link on the left side and looking under Share Statistics for the short percentage of the float. This tells you what percentage of the float—the shares that are listed and publicly traded—has been sold short. If it's high—and I

regard anything over 10 percent as high, and anything over 20 percent as astronomical—you could be set up for either a short squeeze or a big decline. If there's high short interest and the shorts are wrong, you get a short squeeze. (A short squeeze happens when a stock that the shorts expected to decline instead goes up and the shorts decide to cut their losses. In order to do that, they have to buy the stock to cover their short positions. That causes the price of the stock to go even higher.) But when the shorts are right, you see the stock fall. I'd say that the shorts are right about as often as they're wrong. But when the analysts all love a stock that the shorts hate, it's much more likely that the shorts will be right and the stock will go lower. A lot of people expect a short squeeze when they see a high level of short interest, but as you know from this rule, that's often the wrong expectation. When all the analysts love a stock, but it's still heavily shorted, that tells you something is wrong, but no one's talking about it. And in my book, that means sell.

I came up with this rule on July 21, 2006, when I brought on Dan Marino, the former quarterback for the Miami Dolphins and the newest spokesman for NutriSystem (NTRI). When I brought Dan Marino on the show, NTRI was priced at $64.95. After talking to Dan about the company, which makes mail-order low-fat, low-calorie meals to help people lose weight, and about how it was expanding its customer base into the male market, I told people not to buy the thing. The stock was much hyped. All the analysts loved it; Dan Marino was out there telling people how great it was; the company was touting its new men's business; and the stock had become very expensive. But nobody on the Street was talking about how NutriSystem's distribution model, selling meals directly to the consumer without any retail presence, meant that the company's growth would quickly run out. Nobody was discussing the fact that 26.6 percent of the float had been sold short—that's more than a quarter of the shares that were being shorted. There was a large cohort of investors who hated the stock, who thought it would go lower, but none of the people who were talking about the stock in public—the executives, the spokes-man, or even the analysts who are supposed to do the due diligence—ever mentioned that the stock might be overvalued. I said it was too expensive and I got people out. This stock that was at $64.95 when I gave it the thumbs-down went to $54.42 just four days later on July 25 and then to $45 on August 8. I helped you sidestep a 31 percent de-cline over the course of a few weeks because I created this rule: when you see a lot of non-numbers hype, when you see that the analysts love a stock, and you also see that it's heavily shorted, meaning that a lot of well-educated investors hate the thing, that's when you want to sell.

9. Know how to spot downturns in cycles other than the business cycle. I've told you how to spot good cycles like the strength in the aerospace cycle, and I've told you how to examine the business cycle in order to figure out which sectors should be in favor. But I haven't told you how to spot a bad cycle and get out of everything levered to it. It goes without saying that when you catch a stock that's levered to a cycle that's about to start trending downward, you should sell the thing. But how do you know that a cycle like the technology gadget cycle or the telecommunications equipment cycle has started to go bad? The good news for you is that you have a lot of time. It can take three months for the Street to appreciate fully that a good cycle has turned bad, and as long as you're doing the homework and following the right indicators, you can get out too. What are the right indica-tors? Just follow the money. If new orders for airplanes start to de-cline, guess what—the aerospace cycle is running out of steam. If you own Boeing, by the time you learn that those new orders are declin-ing, the stock will already have come down a little. Don't worry, you still have time to get out. It'll go down a whole lot more if the cycle is really slowing.

The best example of this on *Mad Money* has been my treatment of Lucent (LU), a stock I once liked but hated consistently throughout the end of 2005 and 2006. Lucent makes telecommunications equipment, so it's about as levered as a company can be to the telco equipment cycle. From its peak in April 2006 at more than $3, to its latest trough in July and August at slightly more than $2, I was telling you to sell. There were a lot of reasons to hate Lucent, but the thing that really killed the stock, the thing you could have caught, was the slowing of the telco equipment cycle. How could you know this cycle was slowing down before the Street figured it out? You had to be looking for things that tend to slow, or stop, telco spending entirely. You have to look at the phone companies, because they're the guys who spend the money; they buy the telco equipment. In 2006 there were two things that pretty much stopped telco spending dead in its tracks, and at least with the first one, you could have predicted what would happen before the Street did.

The telecommunications sector was seeing a lot of consolidation: AT&T had merged with SBC and they were trying to integrate; Verizon bought MCI and they were trying to integrate; and the merged AT&T/SBC was buying BellSouth. Under ordinary circumstances, all of these companies should have been spending a fortune on telco equipment, because they had to compete with the cable companies and even Internet companies offering phone service over the Web. That's why people continued to hang on to the telco suppliers, stocks like Lucent, through their long decline. But these mergers changed everything. When one company acquires another similar and similarly sized company, it usually takes a few quarters, even a year, to finish integrating the company. During that period of time, the company will spend less money on new equipment as it tries to figure out the shape of its new business. Plus, when a company buys another big company, it doesn't have as much money to spend on new capital. All of these telco mergers dramatically slowed spending on new telco equipment, and that killed Lucent and everything like it.

Then it got even worse when, on July 13, 2006, a federal judge decided to do his job properly and hold up the antitrust settlements between the merging telco companies and the government. He decided he'd make sure there wasn't any monopolistic, anticompetitive behavior going on, and that held up the integration of these phone companies. It also meant that, until they got a decision from this judge, they weren't going to make any big decisions. They were going to hold off on a lot of their new-equipment spending because they had no idea what the future of their business would look like. The judge's decision came at these companies out of nowhere—they pretty much expected that they'd bought and paid for the whole U.S. government, but it turns out they were wrong. Could you have seen this coming? Yeah, if you're a little less cynical than I am, you probably would have expected a judge to have a problem with these mergers, because they *are* monopolistic. Still, the broader point is that mergers between the companies that buy telco equipment, or any other kind of equipment, will slow spending for that equipment and drive down the stocks that supply it. That's an easy way for you to spot a downturn in a cycle that isn't the business cycle and get out while the getting is good.

10. Look out for multiple contraction. When the economy slows down and the Fed raises interest rates, you need to beware of multiple contraction. What is multiple contraction? It's when growth stocks with high P/E multiples—a 30 multiple is high, and anything above 40 is pretty astronomical, although this always depends on growth—get lower multiples during a slowdown, even if they deliver on their earnings and their growth estimates. You'll recall that when a stock gets a lower multiple, it gets cheaper. I can get you out of high-multiple stocks before they experience multiple contraction and lose you money, but you have to follow my instructions. Multiple contraction happens during a slowdown for a number of reasons. First, if the Fed is raising rates, that means people are afraid of inflation. Stocks are mostly valued on the basis of their future earnings, and this is especially true of high-multiple stocks. When you have high inflation, the

value of those future earnings decreases because the value of a dollar a year or two years from now is decreasing—that's the definition of inflation. That's part of why multiple contraction happens. The big reason, though, has more to do with how investors behave, and here again I'm talking mostly about the big institutional hedge funds and mutual funds. During a slowdown the big players don't like to own high-multiple stocks. They feel like they're sticking their necks out if they own something with a P/E of 40, because the economy is slowing and they don't expect most businesses to do very well. The big funds don't have much conviction that these high-multiple stocks can deliver their earnings because of the slowdown. That makes them skittish investors. It means that they'll sell these stocks on the slightest pretexts. During an economic slowdown with rising interest rates (a terrible environment, but a common one because at the beginning of an economic slowdown you still get a lot of inflation), most high-multiple stocks will get crushed when they report their earnings, even if they meet expectations. These companies must beat the expectations, otherwise they'll go down, because in a poor economic environment, their high multiples make them priced for perfection.

The good thing about multiple contraction is that most of these high-multiple stocks don't get really hurt until they actually report their earnings. That means as long as you're aware of the slowdown—and it's not hard to notice a slowdown—then you can get out before the pain starts. This is exactly what happened with Whole Foods (WFMI) and Starbucks (SBUX) in July and August 2006. I had been telling people to sell these stocks during the "Lightning Round" for months before the companies reported their earnings on July 31 (Whole Foods) and August 2 (Starbucks). I told people that given the economic slowdown, these two high-multiple stocks had become priced for perfection, and while they might deliver adequate quarters, perfection was out of the question. Investors in both Starbucks and Whole Foods were scared because they'd seen other high-multiple stocks get cratered and because they thought the slowdown would hurt both of these companies. They were looking for any reason to sell, and I figured they would get it when the companies reported their earnings. These two companies were ripe for multiple contraction, but that didn't occur until after they reported earnings. If you owned them you had at least a month to spot the impending multiple contraction and sell the stock before it happened, because when it happens, it happens all at once. Whole Foods reported on July 31, 2006, and even though earnings were good, same-store sales growth was 9.9 percent when the Street was looking for 10 percent. Because of that microscopic miss, the stock fell from $57.31 to $51.54 overnight—that's 10 percent of its value in an evening. Starbucks reported on August 2. They delivered 4 percent same-store sales growth. They had predicted a range of 3 percent to 7 percent, and the Street was looking for the high end of the range. Once again, overnight Starbucks fell from $33.30 to $29.09, losing more than 12 percent of its value.

Multiple contraction hurts. It's like a hard-to-diagnose cancer. But it can be spotted in time, from afar, before it is fatal, as its most important symptom—interest rates—rise sharply. I told people it was coming whenever they called in about these stocks in the "Lighting Round," and I'll do it again. But now you know how multiple contraction works, and you know to sell high multiple stocks *before* they report earnings during a slowdown, before everyone else sells the stock.

Those are all my new rules that I've created by analyzing my best picks on the show. If you read them carefully and obey them, you should be able to make good stock picks yourself and be able to sell stocks when you see the right indicators. These aren't arbitrary rules. They come from more than a year of hard work and analysis on *Mad Money.* You should take advantage of my experience so you can get the jump on investors who don't have access to it.

10

HOW DO I PICK STOCKS
FOR THE SHOW?

I know if there's one thing you want, it's to be able to figure out which stocks I'm going to recommend before I pick them. People on the Street have started calling this Cramertrage. You want to be able to game Cramer, and why wouldn't you? I can't give you the perfect way to figure out what I'm going to say before I say it; that just doesn't exist. But I can tell you some of the ways I go about picking stocks for the show. That way you can follow the same sources I follow, look at the same things I look at, and maybe reach some of the same conclusions I reach. You've gotta think like I think if you want to beat me to the punch. I can't turn you into me, but I can tell you what I pay attention to.

First, if you want to buy a stock ahead of a recommendation on the show, you should read everything I read. Many of my ideas are ripped straight from newspapers and magazines. If you follow along and read everything that I'm looking at, you should be able to look for ideas that fit into the *Mad Money* mold. So what do I look at? (There's a lot here, and I don't think you have to read everything. You should only do this if you're trying to buy stocks before I recommend them.) I read the *Wall Street Journal,* the *New York Times,* the *Financial Times;* my local paper, Newark's *Star-Ledger; USA Today, Investor's Business Daily* (that produces some of the best ideas out there, and I'll often take mine directly from *IBD*); and everything on TheStreet. com, which I own the biggest chunk of, including all its electronic newsletters. I read the trade publications for a dozen different industries, I read the *Economist,* and most important, I pay attention to Oprah. Don't laugh at that; I'm serious. One of my best calls ever, Deckers (DECK), a stock I recommended on November 30, 2005 came straight out of Oprah. She endorsed their shoes, and I knew that endorsement would translate into big sales. The stock was at $23.03 when I got on it, and five months later on April 28, the stock closed at $42.69. In less than half a year, Oprah gave you an 85 percent gain. That's better than most of the stocks *Investor's Business Daily* picks out. Oprah really counts. She's the biggest force driving the American consumer, and you've gotta pay attention to her if you want to predict my recommendations.

You don't have to read every single publication to try to get the jump on me. That's probably not the most efficient way to do it, although it is the most effective, because it can give you a half-decent picture of all the facts that are buzzing around in my head. If you want to game the show, you're trying to make easy money, and that means you probably don't want to invest all the hard work and effort that it takes to follow every publication that I follow. You want fast and easy tricks to help predict the stocks I'll feature. I have three tricks you can use, if you're that kind of investor.

First trick: I always keep my eyes on the fifty-two-week-high list. I don't usually recommend stocks that are at their fifty-two-week highs—people won't listen to me, they don't feel comfortable buying a stock that looks that expensive. But I do look for stocks that have had a recent pullback from their fifty-two-week high. If you want to game *Mad Money*, you should look for stocks that have recently pulled back from their fifty-two-week highs. That's one big list of stocks I'm looking at. After that, you want to use a little discretion. Did the stock pull back for a good reason, a bad reason, or was it pure profit-taking? If the stock fell for legitimate reasons, I'm not recommending it on *Mad Money*. If it's down for bad reasons, or if you can't find any reason why it should be down, then there's a chance I'll talk about it, particularly if it has fallen in my 5 to 7 percent sweetspot for buying. Then you've got to look at which sector the stock is in. If it's not in a sector I like, then I probably won't mention it. If the stock didn't pull back for a good reason and it passes the sector test, then you might just have your eye on a stock that I'll recommend on the show. Why do I operate like this? I like to look for stocks with momentum, which is why I look at the fifty-two-week-high list, but I'm also a bargain hunter and I want to help you get a discount on good merchandise. With a stock that's just pulled back from its high, as long as the stock has good fundamentals and more reasons to go up, you get the advantage of upward momentum, and you get it at a good price.

The second trick might seem a little self-promotional, but I'm just trying to give you an honest description of how I pick stocks. I'm not trying to sell you anything. I use my charitable trust, www.Action AlertsPlus.com, as a laboratory for the show. If I buy a stock for my charitable trust and it looks like it's going to work out, or it has already performed for me, then the odds are good I'll give it a recommendation on the show. These are the stocks that I've done the most homework on; they're the ones I know and like best. It's only natural that I'd want to own my favorite stocks, and it's also natural that I'd recommend my favorites. Lucky for you, my charitable trust is totally transparent. You can look at it and watch all my trades before they happen on ActionAlertsPLUS.com, which is part of TheStreet.com. Full disclosure here: this is a subscription service that costs you money, and the principal benefit is to the e-mail service, not the portfolio itself, because of my severe restrictions. I'm also the largest shareholder at TheStreet.com. I don't want you to think that I'm just plugging my product here. But this is often how I choose the stocks I recommend.

I want to make this very clear: I will not recommend every stock I own for my charitable trust. If you subscribe to Action Alerts PLUS, you are not paying for inside information about what I'm going to say on the show. You won't get that. Often, I'll buy a stock for my charitable trust a week or two after I recommend it on TV, as I did with News Corp (NWS). That's right, sometimes Action Alerts PLUS lags the show. I wouldn't recommend buying the service just to get an edge on *Mad Money;* that would be a waste of your money. Plus, not every stock I buy for the charitable trust works out. Some of them are big fat losers, and if you were to buy them hoping I'd talk about them on the show, you'd lose a lot of money waiting for something that in some cases is never going to happen. But in general, if I like a stock enough to put my own money behind it, I like it enough to recommend it on the show.

Third trick: just watch the show. There are some sectors that I'm going to like for months, if not years on end. I liked oil since the show started and then turned on it when the commodity peaked at $78. If you pay attention to what I say on the show, then you know where I stand on most sectors. If you're really attentive, you'll also know which stocks I think are best of breed in each sector. I will mention these stocks over and over again. I'll devote multiple segments to them, because they work.

If we go into an economic slowdown and all the recession stocks start to do well, then you can practically bet money that I'll recommend PepsiCo (PEP) and Procter & Gamble (PG), unless they do something in the interim to lose their best-of-breed status. At any given time there are only so many sectors that are working, and within those sectors I have my favorite stocks. As long as you pay attention to the show, you'll know what I'm thinking about those sectors and those stocks. You should be able to predict what I'll do in the near future, because when I've got a good stock on my hands, I recommend it over and over again. It would be irresponsible not to.

I don't recommend trying to game the show as an investment strategy. Even if you use my three tricks, you'll end up spending way too much time trying to figure out which stocks I'm going to mention, and most of the time you'll probably be wrong. And even if you do get it right, and you're trying to game "the Cramer effect," you won't necessarily make much money. Smaller stocks do go up significantly after I recommend them, but as the show has progressed, I've moved away from recommending small-cap stocks. I still do it, because I believe in speculation, but I do it a lot less frequently. If I recommend the stock of a big company, you won't see much of a bounce. PepsiCo is a $100-billion company. If I recommend PepsiCo, the stock might go up a couple of cents—that's no big deal. I think Chevron, a $140-billion company, was up eight cents after hours when I recommended it.

The definition of a bad investment strategy is one that takes a lot of time and effort, rarely produces successful results, and even when it works, you don't make a lot of money. In short, trying to game *Mad Money* is a waste of your time. You'd be better off if you just listened to my advice and did all of your mandatory homework on every stock you buy. I know that homework can be time-consuming and sometimes it can even seem fruitless, but it's the best way out there by far to make money. Trying to guess which stocks I'll get behind before I mention them on the show might seem like an easy, get-rich-quick strategy, but in reality, it won't work well. You'd be lucky to break even playing that game. I know a lot of people want to do it, and I hope that by telling you how hard it is to do, I've discouraged the practice.

11

EVERYTHING YOU EVER WANTED TO KNOW ABOUT MAD MONEY BUT WERE AFRAID TO ASK

I know my show is crazy. I'll say and do a lot of things that probably don't make any sense to the vast majority of people, but they make sense to me. I want to bring you inside my head, in all its insanity, so that you can understand what the heck I'm talking about and what I'm doing when I smash my buttons, or pull out the bowie knife, or toss my chair across the set. On *Mad Money*, I'm not just trying to make you money. I know that if I can't keep you interested in the stock market and interested in the show, you'll never be willing to do the amount of homework necessary to make yourself a lot of money. That's why I try to keep you entertained. But the show can be only so entertaining if you don't know what I'm doing. I take that back; it can be incredibly entertaining if you don't know what I'm doing, but wouldn't you rather be on the inside and understand exactly what's running through my head?

I think you would. That's why I'm giving you a glossary of my little

Cramerisms, an explanation of some of my props, and a button-by-button analysis of my sound-effects machine. I know I throw a lot of stuff out at you when I do the show, but now you'll be part of a small group of people who can actually follow and understand my own personal gibberish.

Glossary of Cramerisms

Booyah: People are constantly asking me where this one came from, because almost every single caller on the show gives me some kind of booyah, or stuttering booyah, or familial booyah with the kids involved as soon as I take their call. I don't know what "booyah" is supposed to mean, although it might be southern for "mazel tov." People started giving me booyahs on my radio show, *Real Money,* well before *Mad Money* had come into existence. Here's the story: someone called up and thanked me for making him a hundred dollars, a hundred points up, on Kmart. This caller was from New Orleans, and he told me the only word they have for making that kind of money down there was "booyah." Then I take the next call, and this guy tells me I also made him a lot of money, and in a much more timid and tentative voice, he says "booyah" too. Ever since, almost everyone who calls into the show gives me a booyah, and I return the favor. It was organic and unprompted. Now I'm the booyah guy, and I don't even really know where it comes from or what it's supposed to mean.

Booyah-free zone: Sometimes I get tired of the booyahs and the chit-chat, and I just want to get to as many stocks as possible. That's why I've declared "Sudden Death," the last segment of my show, which is just like the "Lightning Round," a booyah-free zone. Anyone who gives me a booyah or tries to say anything other than a quick hello and the name of their stock gets buzzed and I move on to the next caller. I know this seems really rude, but I'm trying to get to as many people as possible. There are dozens of people waiting on the line, hoping to ask me about their stocks, and if I don't buzz people for throwing out a booyah in the booyah-free zone, I'll never get to those callers.

The brokers: I misname these guys all the time. Morgan Stanley becomes Mogen David, the kosher wine, because Morgan Stanley is so obviously not a kosher wine. Goldman Sachs becomes Golden Slacks, for no real reason. And Merrill Lynch becomes Merrill Reese, who is the great voice of my beloved Philadelphia Eagles.

The Brothers Johnson: Johnson & Johnson (JNJ).

CNBC alert: When I say this, it means there's no alert. I'm talking about old news.

Gentleman farmer: I call myself a gentleman farmer, in the mold of Thomas Jefferson, all the time on the show. That's because Dan Rather did a piece about me for *60 Minutes,* and in it he called me a gentleman farmer because I have a farm. I liked the sound of that so much that I kept repeating it.

Government of, by, and for the corporation: I mean the United States government whenever I say this. It's a pretty straightforward phrase. I didn't start using it until it became clear that the Bush administration would do almost anything for big business, and those guys weren't even being bribed! Don't get confused: this isn't a political opinion; I keep those off the show. When you've got a government that faithfully serves the needs of its real constituents, big corporations, then it's a lot easier to make money in the market, and that's the purpose of the show. When I say our government is of, by, and for the corporation, I don't mean that as a criticism. It's a compliment.

Mispronunciations: A*von, Chevron,* Pf-izer, Luchent, Von*age*—I mispronounce all of these names. Why? When a company gets it wrong, when they screw up bigtime, they become undeserving of their name, so I either come up with a new one or I accent it the wrong way.

Nokiaah: This is what I call Nokia, the cellular phone company. It's a parody of *tekiah,* the great shofar sound you get to hear on the Jewish high holidays.

Oligopoly, plutocracy, kleptocracy: All things that are good for a shareholder.

Other people want to make friends, I . . . : Every night I like to change this line up, just to keep the show fresh and keep people guessing. It started as "I just want to make money," but that got stale. Now I try out a new catchphrase almost every day.

Rooney McFaddy: This one has to do with my Philadelphia roots. It's a suffix my favorite hometown DJ, Hy Lit, used to tack on to everything for no apparent reason. I'm keeping up the tradition.

Second on CNBC: There are way too many "first on CNBC"s during the day, especially ones that are about stories that are actually second, or third, or fourth on CNBC. I'm just trying to keep myself honest.

Sipping cheap scotch on my dirty linoleum floor: A constant reference to my off-camera, sad-clown home life.

Skip, Captain, Chief, Buddy, Sport, Boss, Champ: All of these are names I call people when they call into the show because they're all the names I was called in my four years hawking Cokes and then ice cream at Veterans Stadium, the former home of the Phillies.

There goes Swifty: This is something I say right at the beginning of "Sudden Death," the last segment on the show, a booyah-free zone.

This reference comes right from my hedge fund. Every morning at 9:30, when the market opens, I'd say, "There goes Swifty" to start the trading. Why? Because it's what they say at the Wonderland dog track when the race starts: Swifty is the fake rabbit the dogs chase. I think the market is about as rational as the dogs, and in a lot of ways, it's not that different from other forms of gambling, so at my hedge fund, I'd treat the stock market like the dog track. I'm a little less cynical these days. I still think the market is totally irrational, but now I know that there are ways you can make money, as long as you stay disciplined, and that's nothing like gambling. Do not confuse this term with the nickname for Swift Transportation, a trucking company I *don't* like.

There's always a bull market somewhere: That's my catchphrase at the end of every show, and it comes from my mantra in my last book, *Jim Cramer's Real Money: Sane Investing in an Insane World*. If you want to know more, you'd better read it.

24: On the show I make almost constant reference to Jack Bauer, President Logan, and President Palmer from *24,* even though *24* airs on a rival network that belongs to a rival company. What can I say? It's the best show on television.

Viginia: This should be Virginia, but my dad and I say "Viginia" because we've got thick, incomprehensible Philadelphia accents.

Wheels of capitalism: When I talk about the wheels of capitalism, I usually tell you that they're greased or powered by the desire for youthful, clear, wrinkle-free skin. That means that in late-stage capitalism—a useful Marxist term for our current mode of production—commerce is driven by vanity. People want to buy things that make them look good or give them social status, and that vanity has become so important that it dominates the economy. Usually when I talk about the wheels of capitalism, it means you should buy Allergan

(AGN), which makes Botox, which takes care of the wrinkles on your forehead, or Medicis (MRX), which makes Restylane, which takes care of the wrinkles below your forehead and doesn't paralyze you from smiling.

Why Do I Do Crazy Things, and What Are the Props For?

Why do I abuse my chair, and sit in it only for "Am I Diversified?"

Chairs are the enemy. When I still worked at my hedge fund, Cramer Berkowitz, I absolutely hated chairs at my desk. Chairs encouraged people to be off their game and focus on other things, like sleep. I would make everyone come in at 6:00 a.m., and if they could, they'd try to pass out in a chair—hey, I am no mean taskmaster. I was in by 4:00 a.m. or I was late! Since I wanted to make money, I needed everyone on top of things, so I had to do away with chairs. On the show I've destroyed so many chairs before the "Lightning Round" that I can't keep count. The first chair hurt my back, and for a while I had a red chair that was too heavy to throw. Lately I've stopped throwing the chair every day, but I still try to find novel ways to attack it.

Why am I the only man on cable news who rolls up his sleeves?

As I've said before, I treat *Mad Money* with the same level of seriousness and intensity that I previously reserved for my hedge fund. At the hedge fund, I kept my sleeves rolled up. Why mess with a good thing?

Why did I burn money on the set when I talked about Chevron?

This was a reference to the second greatest show on television: *The Shield*. It comes from the second-to-last episode of season three, in which Lem, one of the main characters, throws the Armenian money train cash into a furnace. Chevron is equally disdainful of money, or at least it acts that way when it reports.

The Props

The bear in the background: I keep a stuffed bear in the background, off my desk and away from the camera, because when I gave the bear center stage one night, the show got bad ratings. The bear has been relegated to the background as punishment.

Bobble-head dolls: I keep a few Cramer bobble heads on set because they're fun to decapitate when I'm having a bad day, or when the market's been hit hard. You can buy them at the NBC Experience Store, order them online at www.ShopMadMoney.com, or pay an outrageous price for one on eBay.

The Book: Actually this refers to both *Jim Cramer's Real Money: Sane Investing in an Insane World* and *Confessions of a Street Addict.* I like to keep both books on the set for more shameless self-promotion, and because the wall makes cool sound effects whenever I throw the book at it. I usually give you my current Amazon ranking at the same time.

Bowie knife: I bring this out whenever I need a little extra emphasis.

Bulls and bears on the set: I keep these around because they're easy to chop, fillet, and dice for emphasis.

Cramerica banner: I keep this banner on the backs of all my computers because a viewer sent me a whole package of them. If you send me interesting stuff about the show, the odds are good that it'll get on television.

Lesser Evil Popcorn: I keep at least a box of this on set because I'm a partner in the privately held company that makes it. More shameless self-promotion.

Mad Money baseball bat: It's a necessity when you want to smash things, and on *Mad Money*, we want to smash things.

Mad Money blanket and pillows: I keep these around so that I can take a nap on the floor whenever I get a really long-winded caller.

Picture of Che Guevara: I keep the picture of Che around because he's the ultimate enemy of capitalism, and I think it's hilarious that he's become an icon, given that he was a Stalinist and a nut *and* part Irish! The picture of Che helps keep my show fair and balanced.

The Portrait of Cramer as a Middle-Aged Man: I stuck this painting of myself in the back of the set for two big reasons: one, it's a great painting, and two, it's a Gene Hackman painting, and he's the greatest American actor out there and a damned good artist. I will use every opportunity on the show to make gratuitous references to Gene Hackman. Feel free to turn that fact into a drinking game.

Quogue Market hat: I keep this hat on set because hats rate. The same is true for the football helmet, the sombrero, and hats made by various retailers I reference. For some reason, people like to see hats on TV, and I give the people what they want. They have a great chicken salad on pita at the Quogue Market.

Real Money soda: This stuff is actually Jones Soda, but a viewer changed the labels and sent me the bottles.

Red flag: I toss out the red flag as a coach's challenge when someone says something that I know is absolutely, factually incorrect. If you call in and say something that just plain isn't true, you get a red flag.

Yellow flag: This one is for unsportsmanlike hyping. Whenever some-one calls in to plug a stock they own, especially a small-cap stock, I'll give them a yellow flag. Phone calls are for questions, not for hyping stocks you already own.

The Buttons

I try to rotate through my sound effects, creating new buttons and tossing out some of the sounds that have gotten stale. Now I'll give you a list of what I have on my sound-effects board right now, and what each of those buttons means for you whenever I hit it.

Row One

Bull: The bull means you buy.

Bear: The bear means you sell.

Ka-ching: I usually use the *ka-ching* noise, which is cash-register sound, to tell you to ring the register and take profits in a stock you own that's gone up.

Bowling pins: This button is for pin action. What's pin action? It's when something happens to one company that affects a whole lot of other stocks. The media doesn't ever report on the pin action, they just tell the straight story. We like pin action, because stocks that get pin action are stocks with good news that the market hasn't noticed yet. I always say "Courtesy of the Plaza Lanes in Madison" because those are the lanes where I like to bowl. I do have my own shoes and bowling ball. Don't you?

Shotgun: Come on, you've gotta have a shotgun.

Triple-sell: Sell the stock with great enthusiasm.

Train wreck: I use the train wreck button to indicate that either a stock or a company has become a train wreck, in which case it's lost people a lot of money and you should stay away, or it's on track to become a train wreck.

Man out window: This button could be about a stock that's taking a plunge. It could be about an analyst who got a stock so wrong that he's probably thinking about heading out the window. It could be me after I make a really big mistake on the show. In confession, I fantasized about taking the plunge, but decided it might be premature.

Row Two

'Mon back: When I hit this button it means you've gotta back up the truck and load it up with whatever stock I'm talking about.

Buzzer: I use the buzzer in "Sudden Death." If someone breaks the rules, if I hear a booyah in the booyah-free zone, you get buzzed and I move on to the next caller.

Hogs: When I hit this button you hear the sweet sound of pigs getting slaughtered. Remember my mantra: bulls make money, bears make money, pigs get slaughtered. If I give you the hog button, it means you're getting greedy by hanging on to a stock that's already made you a lot of money. Originally this was the pigs button, but then someone e-mailed me and explained that a hog is a domesticated pig that you slaughter. I think "hogs get slaughtered" loses some of the punch of the original catchphrase. Oh, and hogs are much dumber than pigs— which can actually be taught to understand three hundred words!

"Stars and Stripes Forever": When I play "The Stars and Stripes Forever" on the show, it's to celebrate our government of, by, and for the corporation because it makes us so much money.

House of pleasure: A stock puts you in the house of pleasure when it's making you money and there's more money to come. The voice is the voice of Laura Koski, my excellent makeup artist and a Tupelo Honey to boot.

Ghost: This is my newest button as I write this book, and I use it to make fun of panicked journalists, analysts, and investors who get scared by the dumbest things.

Horse race: I hit this button when a stock is off to the races. It's going much higher, and it's getting there fast. It's also the sound that lets you know the "Lightning Round" has begun.

"Hallelujah Chorus": You know how it feels when you own a stock that's been hammered and at long last it starts turning around and making you money—that deserves a hallelujah. I use this button even though the sound effect comes from Handel's *Messiah*, and Handel was a total hack.

Row Three

Applause: The applause button goes to an analyst who gets something right, a company that does something right, or in a rare moment of self-praise, to me for nailing a stock.

Gong: Most of you are probably too young to remember *The Gong Show*, but when something or someone gets gonged that's because it's so bad that it doesn't even deserve our attention anymore. I also use the gong at random moments, mostly for emphasis. And, of course, I gong the Chinese Communist stocks, which I don't care for.

Flatline: This is the sound of an EKG machine flatlining, the sound the machine makes when the person it's hooked up to dies. If a stock gets the flatline button, get out fast.

Head chop: I hit this button to produce the sound of a guillotine chopping someone's head off. It's a versatile button. It could apply to a bad stock, a disgraced analyst, a disgraced Jim Cramer, or a dozen other things. Generally, you don't want to get your head chopped off, so it usually means you should sell something.

Baby: The sound of a baby crying is another really versatile button. I'll use this button to show you how an analyst feels after he gets something really wrong and takes a lot of heat for it, usually from me. But the button can also dismiss and ridicule the alleged "pain" someone feels when he owns a stock that's gone down a percent or two.

Triple-buy: Buy the stock with great enthusiasm.

Don't buy: This is a tepid button. I hit it when I don't like a stock, but when the stock is not bad enough to warrant a sell. On Wall Street, when they don't want you to buy or sell a stock, they give it a hold. But calling a stock a hold is much more positive sounding than it should be. Hold means don't buy, and I like to cut to the chase.

House of pain: If you've spent much time owning stocks, you know what the house of pain feels like. I hit this button to emphasize just how terrible a stock has been to its shareholders.

Row Four

Machine gun: When the machine gun gets going, that can mean one of three things. I don't want you to be confused and get hit with friendly fire. When I hit this button sometimes I'm taking heavy fire: maybe a stock I like is going down or being attacked or someone is panning me in the press. On the other hand, I might be the guy operating the imaginary machine gun and pointing it at an ugly stock or an analyst who's so wrong we need to mount a full frontal assault to get rid of his or her advice. The third possibility is that I'm talking about a battleground situation, a situation where too many companies are competing with one another and nobody can make money. In that case, you want to stay away, just as you would have stayed away from Verdun in 1916, one of the bloodiest battles in human history. Or the first day of the Somme, when nearly 60,000 British soldiers were killed or wounded attacking well-entrenched, well-armed Germans.

Ta-dah: When I'm teasing you guys by touting a stock but holding back on what it is, I hit this button before I tell you the stock's name. I like to keep things theatrical, if not histrionic.

Submarine dive: When I hit this button, a submarine captain shouts "Dive." Then you know the stock I'm talking about is going much lower. I will also reference *Run Silent, Run Deep,* which is the best World War II naval movie, including *Sink the Bismarck!* and *Tora! Tora! Tora!*

Dog: While theoretically the dog button, which makes the sound of a dog barking, could refer to any really bad stock, it almost always refers to just one: Vonage, the worst-performing IPO of at least the first half of 2006 and a company that truly deserves the dog label. You never, ever want to own a stock that's a dog. I'll be honest, I've always been a cat person, having at one time cleaned the litter boxes of Fang, Dinah, Cuzie, Nemo, Iverson, Buddy, and Happy.

Boo: If anyone or any company ever does anything I don't like, all I have to do is hit a button and a whole crowd of people will boo at them. Since I'm an even-handed guy, I make the crowd boo at me just as often as anyone else.

Da whip: When don't I use da whip? I can use it for self-flagellation if I get something wrong, or if I'm just down on myself for no particular reason. I can use it to whip a bad stock or a bad analyst. But the best thing about da whip is that it works so well with my other sound effects. The dog, and then da whip. The crying baby, and then da whip. Da whip followed by the gong. The list goes on. If any one button is essential for me to be able to communicate with you guys, it's this one.

Chime: When opportunity rings the doorbell, I hit this button and you buy that opportunity.

Jackhammer: A stock gets the jackhammer when it's being totally pounded into dust by the market. When you hear this sound you know that I'm predicting pain and demolition. Only the toughest, most emotionless investors can handle a stock that's getting jackhammered, and most of them shouldn't even try, because it doesn't make sense to take any pain if you can avoid it.

STOCK WORKSHEET

STEP ONE: **Find out how the company makes it money.**

How did it make its money last year?

How did it make money last quarter?

Are these high- or low-quality earnings?

STEP TWO: **What sector does the company belong to and how has that sector performed?**

Sector:

Sector performance over the last three, six, and twelve months:

What forces tend to move stocks in this sector?

STEP THREE: How has the stock performed?

Last year:

Last six months:

Last three months:

Last month:

Last week:

STEP FOUR: What do the comparisons tell you?

Does this company face any threatening competition?

What is the P/E of this stock?

What is the average P/E of its competitors?

What is the PEG rate of this stock?

What is the average PEG rate of its competitors?

How much cheaper or more expensive is this stock compared to its peers?

Based on P/E:

Based on PEG:

STEP FIVE: Can the stock survive its balance sheet?

How much debt does this company have?

How much debt does it have due this year?

How much free cash flow did the company have last year?

How much free cash flow should it have this year according to analyst estimates?

Will this company generate enough cash flow to pay its debts this year?

Can it pay its debts next year?

Will it have to sell assets to pay its debts in the near future?

STEP SIX: Does this stock look like a good investment in light of your homework?

CYCLICAL INVESTING UPDATE

In my last book, *Real Money,* I included a chart that I would use at my hedge fund. This chart tells us what stocks to buy and sell depending on where we are in the business cycle. In the year and a half since the creation of *Mad Money,* I've made a handful of alterations to the chart as I've learned new things and adapted to new circumstances. I'd be a pretty poor source of advice if I didn't give you these alterations in the form of a revised chart, so here it is.

Updated Cyclical Investing and Trading

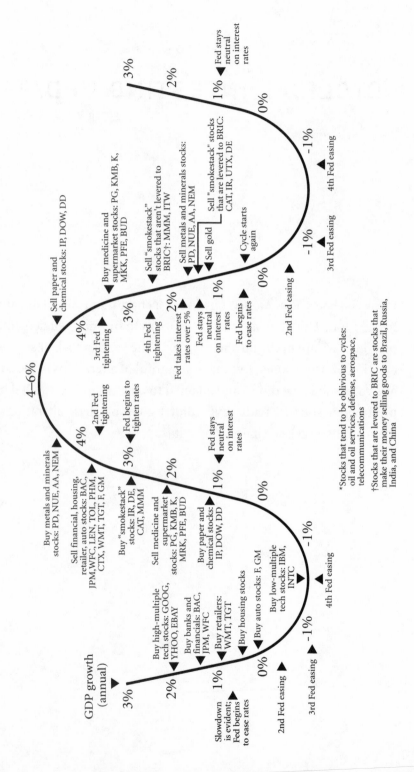

ACKNOWLEDGMENTS

The most important person behind this book and the show that made it necessary is you. Everything I do in my professional life, I do for you and people like you. *Mad Money* is a two-way street. I learn as much from you as you do from me. I don't want to call anyone a fan of *Mad Money*, because I don't think I have fans, I have collaborators. You're trying to make money, and I try to make that process a little less difficult, a little less perplexing, a little less frustrating. To everyone who's ever called in to *Mad Money* or written me an e-mail, whether it's to ask a question, toss out an idea, or tell me I'm an idiot: thank you. You make me better at what I do, and that in turn helps everyone else who's listening.

I wouldn't be here, writing this book or standing in the middle of your television, without a giant support network, and everyone in it has my immense gratitude. Once again, I need to thank Tom Clarke, the truly incredible CEO of TheStreet.com, for making it all possible, along with Dave Peltier, Jonathan Edwards, Michael Comeau, Frank Curzio, Gretchen Lembach, and Dave Morrow, who are my brain trust at TheStreet.com.

Mad Money is a team effort, and neither the show nor this book would be possible without the superlative efforts of Rich Flynn, Jackie

DeAngelis, Dan Hoffman, Morgan Korn, Ben Rippey, George Manessis, Joanna Chow, Chris Schwartz, Mike Waller, Maria Centrella, Bryan Russo, Keith Greenwood, Jeff Gurnari, Henry Fraga, Dan Hart, Cal Anthony, Kareem Bynes, Kevin Hillard, Sean Riley, and last but not least, Regina Gilgan, who deserves much of the credit for taking a good show and making it fantastic.

This book would not exist without Suzanne Gluck, the best literary agent bar none, and Henry Reisch, who's been inspirational as a big-thinking, get-it-done agent.

As always, enormous thanks are due to Bob Bender, the best financial editor in the world, and David Rosenthal, who is the reason I write books to begin with.

INDEX